CRISIS
OF
CLARITY

Previous books by Michael Bradley

Novels

The Mantouche Factor
Imprint

Non-Fiction

The Cronos Complex I
The Iceman Inheritance

CRISIS OF CLARITY

The New Democratic Party and the Quest for the Holy Grail

by Michael Bradley

Summerhill Press Ltd.
Toronto

Published by: Summerhill Press Ltd.
Toronto, Ontario

The publisher has made every effort to give accurate credit to the sources of quotations which appear in this book. In the event of error or omission, notification would be appreciated.

Canadian Cataloguing in Publication Data

Bradley, Michael, 1944-
  Crisis of clarity

Bibliography: p.
ISBN 0-920197-20-5

1. New Democratic Party. I. Title.

JL197.N48B73   324.27107   C85-099395-4

Distributed in Canada by:
Collier Macmillan Canada
50 Gervais Drive
Don Mills, Ontario M3C 3K4

Printed and bound in Canada by John Deyell Company

For
Deanna Taheilmann-Bean
and
Jason

Contents

Foreword

Throughout this book, just as during every provincial and federal election, it will prove impossible to escape terms like "Liberal" and "Conservative" and the supposedly differing "political philosophies" these parties represent. Yet, in tracing the long defeat of the Social Democratic Movement in Canada, it should become clear that neither the Liberals nor the Conservatives represent a political philosophy in the same way that the old CCF and more recent NDP represent one.

In fact, it is the *argument* of this book that the political failure of both CCF and NDP stems directly from the fact that the Social Democratic Movement in Canada did, and still does, derive from a real political philosophy. The corollary to this proposition must be that the Liberals and Progressive Conservatives have tasted success, simply because they do not represent political philosophies at all.

And a further corollary unavoidably suggests itself.

Contemporary Canadian political, economic and cultural crises, which surely must be obvious to everyone with open eyes in 1985, reflect a Canadian inability to recognize what does (and does not) constitute genuine political philosophy, and our national inability or unwillingness to weigh regional, national and international issues within a larger view of human nature and the best sort of society that can be achieved given that nature.

In short, the conclusion indicated by taking a look at fifty years of failure by the CCF and NDP to attain more power in Canadian government must be that this failure is symptomatic of a more profound Canadian failing.

But this conclusion does not mean that this book is necessarily "pro-NDP", or that Social Democrats *should have been* elected to a greater share of political power on the merits of their "superior" political philosophy. What this conclusion implies is something a bit less partisan and a good deal more subtle: that by denying the CCF and NDP a greater degree of political clout the Canadian electorate has avoided a normal stage of political maturation.

Canada, almost uniquely among Western parliamentary democracies, has failed to elevate Social Democratic ideology to Government or Official Opposition after a period of serious political soul-searching. The rest of the Commonwealth did pass through this phase, with Social Democratic governments coming to power in Britain, Australia and New Zealand, and in most non-Commonwealth Western democracies, with the significant exception of the United States.

Our sister nations endured their phase of Social Democratic political cocksure and economic acne to emerge, on the other side, with a more balanced social perspective borne of genuine experience and sincere philosophical conflict.

Politicians of Grit and Tory bent, and political analysts representing Canadian conventional wisdom, will doubtless prefer to believe (as they always have) that Canada escaped an embarrassingly gangly phase of social, political and economic growth thanks to Canada's preference for compromise and conciliation. But then, in grasping this comfortable model of Canadian political evolution, conventional wisdom must account for our seemingly chronic unemployment, our increasingly devalued currency, our cultural stagnation and our irrelevance in the global community — and all this toward the end of a century that was supposed to belong to Canada.

Another way of explaining our contemporary crises is to view them as the culmination of many confrontations that were never resolved, many painful and adventurous socio-political experiences shirked. In other words, Canada as Baby Doll, pre-adolescent politically and economically, clinging to the pseudo-adulthood of the precociously pubescent. In this view of Canadian development, we have failed to reach social, political and economic maturity.

Canada's Social Democratic Movement offered us the opportunity, if only we had had the collective stature to grasp it, of easing our country into global relevance and contribution.

As a nation, we recoiled, preferring the security of a social and political nursery. It is softened by stuffed-toy political leaders with improbable eyes and pretty profiles, whether our favourite teddy is named John Turner or Brian Mulroney. They utter mechanical messages conforming to our regional identities whenever we wind them up for elections.

No great grasp of objectivity is required on my part to realize that this interpretation of Canadian political maturity is likely to prove unpopular with readers and reviewers, however, my past political involvements have allowed me to see, first hand, the game playing that goes on.

I have been associated with the NDP, including being a delegate to the founding convention in 1961 and holding several youth-oriented offices during the early 60s, such as President of the NDP on campus at Dalhousie University in 1964, and President of Toronto NDP youth. Also, I have served as something of a promotional (speech-writing) mercenary for various candidates of the other two parties, mostly PCs. These experiences merely reinforced a growing conviction that Grit and Tory politics were even further removed from any remotely constructive intent than NDP politics.

Current political, social and economic crises of Western civilization are generally regarded as the ongoing collision between "free enterprise" and various reactions against inhumane aspects of it. Those who have sought to limit adverse social repercussions of free enterprise have, during the past century, done so from positions based on Karl Marx's analysis of capitalism. In modern Western democracies, original Marxism has evolved, and softened, into a very ill-defined socio-political philosophy most often called "neo-Marxism". It has been this neo-Marxist social and political philosophy which has, in one form or another, negotiated, by confrontation, the dilution of free enterprise in all modern Western states. The so-called "mixed economy" composed of both free enterprise and government intervention, plus social welfare guarantees to a greater or lesser extent, have been the result in all modern Western nations.

Marxism, and its evolved offspring, neo-Marxism, define human society as basically an economic construct and regard human history as the slow but inevitable process of ever greater numbers of people becoming more equitably enfranchised within that economic construct. This is the ongoing "class struggle" of original Marxism. It was certainly a more scientific and pragmatic model of human nature, society and history than had ever been offered before. Marx proposed a mechanism, economics, to explain human social evolution, just as Charles Darwin had earlier proposed a mechanism to explain human physical evolution. Marx himself recognized his debt to Darwin and wanted to dedicate *Capital* to him. Darwin, however, already had enough troubles and managed to avoid this back-handed compliment.

By the early 1960s it was becoming increasingly apparent to some people that just as Darwinism didn't explain biological evolution without sweeping a great deal under the rug, Marxism (or neo-Marxism) couldn't explain human social evolution and the pattern of human history without leaving a comparable sub-carpet mess.

There was mounting evidence that human social structure and the basic pattern of human history itself were not only the result of conscious effort and more or less mechanical class struggle, but might also be dictated to a significant degree by psychological tendencies imprinted upon humanity because of biolgical evolution.

The scientists who provided this evidence were students of animal behaviour, people like J.C. Braddock, C.R. Carpenter and Konrad Lorenz. They pointed out that much supposedly "human" behaviour in history and society is mirrored in the animal world where similar, or even identical, antics are motivated by biological determinates. The animal behaviourists began to wonder, perhaps irreverently, how much of human behaviour might be motivated by "unconscious" biological imperatives which might act to compromise our supposedly conscious and willful social constructs.

This new view of human nature, society and history came to be called *psychobiology* by some and *sociobiology* by others. It somewhat shyly tendered an explanation as to why almost all human institutions and endeavours have evolved toward counter-productivity and what we like to call "inhumanity"... why, for instance, capitalism and free enterprise have been plagued by a cycle of peace-with-recession alternating with war-and-recovery economics; and why, for instance, Marxism applied in practice has proved a tyranny, while neo-Marxism applied in practice has so often resulted in economic and cultural stagnation instead of human fulfillment.

In the early 1960s I had a budding suspicion that psychobiology (or "sociobiology") would supercede 19th Century Darwinism and Marxism in much the same way that Einstein's physics of relativity had superceded the mechanics of Newton. This suspicion prevented me from taking party politics as seriously as others did, whether among New Democrats, Liberals or Conservatives. It seemed probable to me that psychobiology "beneath" human nature might be more important in determining social reality than so-called "consciously" derived policies based on professed ideology.

This book, in some areas, will attempt to examine the way in which non-traditional political determinants have been a force in past Canadian politics, and how they might still play a role in future changes in the political scene.

Take, for example, the assimilation of Liberal and PC ideologies into a grey mass, which today makes the policies of the two parties virtually indistinguishable. They have had the foresight to realize that the way to succeed in Canadian politics is not to boldly set new directions and risk failure, but to appease the masses, adapt whatever policy the winds of change bring to them, much the same way as any biological creature on this earth seeks to survive, by adapting to a changing environment. The CCF and NDP, on the other hand, in to trying directly confront fundamental problems, have promoted irritation and rejection on the part of the environment (the Canadian voters), and have struggled to survive. The Social Democratic Movement's failure in Canada is in part due to its inability to recognize its own malady, and to begin the cure leading to health and growth.

It is significant that the influence of the NDP as a political force has steadily eroded since the war — since the NDP adopted a policy of neo-Marxism patterned after the British Labour Party. The NDP's greatest successes have occurred when it was perceived as a party of the people, concerned primarily with human suffering and injustice. The humanist policies of CCF founders, such as Tommy Douglas, stuck a resonate chord with concerned Canadian voters. Today, that compassionate political perspective has been lost by the NDP, and its popularity has subsequently declined. Can a return to some of the basic values of the original CCF platform again stir a positive response from voters? This is one of the questions this book will attempt to answer.

Chapter One

Election — 1984

At least as far as Toronto was concerned, there was nothing particularly supernatural or uncanny about the evening of September 4, 1984. But appearances can be deceptive. An event of great interest to spiritualists was in the making.

Drizzle, which had threatened according to forecasts, had held off, and the evening was clear and crisp with the thermometer at a bracing but comfortable 14 Celsius. Not too hot, maybe just a bit cool, which was just right under the circumstances. Like everybody else across Canada, Torontonians were packing themselves into living rooms and friendly bars where they could watch the election returns on television. The cool of the evening made the heat tolerable, and there was a lot of heat, not only from the sheer press of bodies, but from their emotion.

All across the country there was great anticipation, not to say salivation, although the prey had (and not for the first time) managed to elude the full brunt of Canadians' righteous indignation.

The packs staring at thousands of television screens had, of course, just one emotional focus: savage rejection of Pierre Elliott Trudeau and the party he had led for sixteen years. Canadians everywhere but Quebec had been looking forward to mauling Trudeau at the polls.

But the fox had cheated the hounds while losing little more than a few tufts of prestige from his aristocratic plume. Deftly avoiding inevitable carnage at the polls, Trudeau retired with some dignity, graciously permitting hopeful successors to fight it out among themselves for the dubious privilege of being ravaged in the next election. On the afternoon of June 16, 1984, John Turner fielded the leadership baton on the second ballot, although many felt it was the dirty end of a political stick that he had grasped. As the dogs of political retribution wheeled in pursuit of the surrogate Trudeau had so thoughtfully provided, old Br'er Fox he doubled back and went to earth in Quebec where he watched, with considerable disdain (and not a few hints to the baying pack) the flying fur of his long-time political rival. It had been a tough and hopeless campaign run for John Turner.

As a harried John Turner finally fletched up against the thorny dead end of election night you didn't have to be Martin Goldfarb to scent political blood on the wind.

While ordinary Canadians congregated in front of TV screens at home or in cozy lounges, content, perhaps, to keep track of the popular vote and results from their own ridings, those more directly involved in the fray gathered to whoop and cheer at every slash and tear inflicted on the Liberal body politic.

Tory campaign workers converged on their candidates' victory headquarters with all the enthusiasm of medieval Iberians sprinting to catch sight of an *auto da fe.*

Still in all, there was a cautious quality about their confidence. Tory workers were sure of victory, but uncertain about its magnitude. They hoped for a Mulroney majority, and thought it was in the bag, but were willing to cheer even a minority government. Such is the stigma of failure.

Tory throngs descending on North Toronto Memorial Gardens were typical. It was the victory headquarters of Barbara McDougall, Progressive Conservative candidate in Metro Toronto's St. Paul's riding. I had been invited to attend the celebration, as a sort of mascot with a checkered political past, by two true-blue Tory poll captains of my acquaintance, Susan Leeming and Ellen Dooley. As we walked along Eglinton Avenue toward the unlikely temple where the rites of victory would soon, doubtless, be celebrated, we chatted about the prospects.

As front line workers, Ellen and Susan were justifiably optimistic because of the warm reception McDougall's candidacy had generated among the constituents of St. Paul's riding. They had no doubt that Barbara McDougall would unseat Liberal incumbent, John Roberts, and they had no doubt that Tories would win generally across the nation, but they were unwilling to make excessive estimates of how many seats the Progressive Conservatives might take of the 282 available.

When John Turner had at last bitten the polling bullet and had called the 1984 election, party standings from the outcome of February 18, 1980 were: Liberals 147, PCs 103 and NDP 32. Susan plunked for a modest Tory majority government in 1984, with the PCs taking maybe 150 to 155 seats, the Liberals somewhere about 100 with the NDP taking from 30 to 35. Susan saw a mirror-image of 1980. Ellen thought that the Tories might do a little better, but wouldn't commit herself to numbers.

The slight shadow over their optimism was a somewhat lackluster Sword of Damocles wielded by Ed Broadbent of the NDP. In rejecting the Liberals, which was inevitable, how much of the electorate would swing to the NDP? Although they may have forgotten it by now, on the night of September 4, 1984 at lot of Tory campaign workers in urban ridings were troubled by the possible Liberal/NDP split.

Inside the Memorial Gardens buildings, after we had bellied up to the bar brandishing Susan's and Ellen's campaign spoils in the form of beer and wine tickets, and after our first calming gulps, we cocked our ears to the pre-return buzz of conversation in the room. As an under-current in the crowd's speculations, one caught snatches of continuing concern about the NDP. Mumblings amid the tinkling of plastic cups were that the New Democrats might cop the protest vote and, since the whole country was protesting, that vote could be unexpectedly large indeed. It could mean, horror of horrors, a Tory minority government, with the NDP holding the balance of power — like the short-lived Clark government of 1979 when Liberals and NDP between them could muster 140 MPs to the Tories' 136.

And *that* would inevitably mean a swift return to the political wilderness after a few short months in power. John Turner would oil up the seemingly implacable Liberal machine and start its inexorable clanking once again, and the PCs would again be ground into oblivion. That had been the pattern in 1963 when Pearson had ended the Diefenbaker era, and the pattern in 1979 when Trudeau had done the same for Clark.

Minority governments seemed always to foreshadow the end of too-brief Tory ascendancy in Canadian politics, while perversely heralding the beginning of long-lasting Liberal regimes. Tories had come to hate minority government even more than outright defeat, because *their* minority governments prolonged the agony of inevitable eclipse. The cruel instrument causing Tory pain in minority had been the NDP.

And, ominously, the NDP had steadily increased its power. It was still a minor party, and a protest one, but it was now established. Its power increased proportionately with electoral dissatisfaction. In the first election after its founding in 1961 the NDP had taken 19 seats.

During the years of Trudeaumania and a healthy economy, the NDP stabilized in the 16 to 22 seat range.

But.

As disenchantment with Trudeau deepened, and as the economy deteriorated, New Democrats improved their parliamentary position. In the election of 1979 they took 26 seats, in 1980 they took 32.

Now, on the night of September 4, 1984, with the economy stalled, unemployment high and the value of the dollar falling, and with electoral dissatisfaction at a crescendo of anti-Liberal and anti-Trudeau sentiments, how many votes and how many ridings might drift to the NDP?

No one knew.

In the densely inhabited McDougall victory headquarters, speculative rumours had it that the NDP might take 50 seats, or even 60, enough to make one of those dreaded Tory minority governments likely. It was as if young Tory workers had been reading the mind of Jim Laxer, but taking it more seriously than the NDP ever did.

There seemed to be a pattern, much like handwriting, on the wall and full of portentious messages for everyone able to read it. Because of my past association with the NDP and other parties, which conferred a sort of bogus insider's over-view in the minds of Susan and Ellen, they invited me to attempt a decipherment of the patterns and join the pre-return guessing sweepstakes.

Aside from the numbers game of previous election results, I saw other patterns on the wall. There seemed to be an overpowering other-force at work in this particular election. It emanated from the lower St. Lawrence, near Baie Comeau, in the far-away riding of Manicouagan. Something uncanny had happened to Brian Mulroney. Somehow...he had *become* Mackenzie King. Luckily, my long-standing interest in the occult and spiritualism allowed me to recognize the strange power at work on this election night. The power of political reincarnation.

My scribbled figures quickly materialized on a McDougall cocktail-napkin, like automatic writing: PCs 195, Liberals 45 and NDP 42.

A majority government for the Tories, almost as big a sweep as

Dief's great victory of March 31, 1958. Susan's and Ellen's partisan sentiments were relieved, but not quite convinced.

About that time the clock struck eight, the polls closed and television volume was turned up as the networks began feeding the East Coast returns. Of the 32 seats in the four Atlantic provinces, Tories were leading or elected in 25. Newfoundland had the most even split, with PCs taking 4 and the Liberals taking 3 seats. But the other three Maritime provinces reflected the sweep: Tories 9, Liberals 1 in New Brunswick; Tories 3, Liberals 1 in Prince Edward Island; Tories 9, Liberals 2 in Nova Scotia.

As the evening wore on, Memorial Gardens was rocked by cheers as Tory after Tory was elevated to the Commons, and Liberal after Liberal was cast down to ignominious defeat. Yet, for all the cheering, the victorious crowd was subdued. One couldn't help thinking that a closer contest would have generated more noise. Even the inevitable rendition of "Happy Days Are Here Again" was less boisterous than might have been expected. The truth was that the young Tory workers at Barbara McDougall's celebration were stunned, just like other young PCs across the nation, by the scope of the political debacle they had wrought. My own prediction of 195 PC seats, only hopefully half-believed before the television volume was turned up, proved niggardly indeed.

But, for all that, the prediction was more accurate than others. Even Martin Goldfarb, clearly a bit uncertain when interviewed on television before the East Coast polls began to report, guessed that the Tory total might be around 190 seats.

No one anticipated what was to be the greatest landslide in Canadian political history. By midnight eve, PC workers had accepted the incredible fact that 211 Tories had been elected out of a total of 282 ridings. The Liberals retained only 40 seats, mostly in Quebec, and the NDP *lost a couple of seats to end up with a total of 30.*

What happened to the NDP? Why had the pattern of its growth become unravelled in the biggest protest election in Canada's history?

The answer is simple — in retrospect. The NDP's growth pattern collided with another pattern — a web of political analysis woven in the shrewd brain of Brian Mulroney. It was not altogether different in shape from the construct of Jim Laxer, which NDP ideologues had dismissed as cobwebs.

Chapter Two

Brian Mulroney:

Politics of Reincarnation

Election night '84 was not a mere repetition of history in spite of superficial resemblance to John Diefenbaker's great victory of 1958 and Joe Clark's lesser one of 1979.

Canadian voting patterns during the 20th Century have institutionalized a strong, if stormy, marriage with the Liberal Party from what had been a 19th Century flirtation with Reform. Since settling down to domesticity in 1921, the Canadian electorate has demonstrated its fidelity to Liberalism by keeping it in power for roughly 52 of the last 64 years, ample time for the Liberals to take their electoral help-mate for granted and develop superb corruption, cynicism and arrogance. It has been the kind of marriage that produces battered wives, as Canada's economic and cultural bruises testify all too clearly, but still her people have run away from Liberalism only three times. These extra-marital flings have been of short duration: five years between 1930 and 1935, six years between 1957 and 1963, and less than two years since 1979.

None of these brief excursions into temporary Tory arms have been sincere attempts to correct a restrictive domestic reality, but rather were pathetic attempts to inspire short-lived jealousy within the heart of the Liberal spouse. The forlorn hope seems to have been to provoke self-evaluation of Liberal conscience, to curb intolerable Liberal arrogance. and it has always worked — for a while. The Liberal Party has hung its head in mock contrition, has proffered sweets and sweet-talk to Canada's regions ... and the country has crawled back home to endure yet more years of deep-seated dissatisfaction.

The nine-month fling with Joe Clark's minority government (May 22, 1979 to February 18, 1980) was typical. If Canadians cannot remember clearly how bad things were then, it is only because things are so much worse now. But, back in 1979, in what may prove to have been the good old days, unemployment was high, inflation was high, Trudeau was believed to have undermined the power of Parliament, he seemed unconcerned about the economy (probably, Canadian felt, because his personal fortune insulated him from hard times) and Margaret's first book, *Beyond Reason,* had just been published.

The opinion samplings had shown that Canadians were furious at Trudeau ... thought he was indifferent to their troubles and arrogant because of his wealth, the privileged playboy husband of a silly, privileged playgirl.[1]

And Canadians were appalled at the falling value of their dollar. It was worth about 90¢ in U.S. currency.

Opposing Trudeau was the earnest, boyish and unpolished Joe Clark with his Tory platform of reducing government spending to slow inflation and his pledge to re-acquaint Ottawa with parliamentary democracy. Canadians rewarded his sincerity and obvious good intentions with a minority government. It might have been a stronger mandate had not the Liberals begun their "fix" immediately. In action if not in words, Trudeau apologized for his arrogance. On the campaign trail he spoke seriously with no trace of flip. In the Commons he suddenly became respectful, concerned. Gone were the days when he mouthed "fuck you" toward Opposition benches. Canada seemed almost mollified before election day. Within nine months, Trudeau was again Prime Minister and the Liberals were again the government.

The country was no better off, and the Liberals did not propose any new policies to make it so, and things continued to deteriorate into the situation in which we find ourselves today. But, at least, Trudeau and the Liberals *appeared* to be serious and concerned, doing their best. And part of the Liberal "fix" involved making Joe Clark *appear* to be inept, putting the worst complexion on his admitted inexperience... "Making Clark look like a hesitant bumbler: that was their goal."[2] It was enough to return them to power.

The "Clark Episode", providing as it did a kind of focused object lesson in the basic Canadian political relationship, held the secret of Canadian political success. Among non-Liberals, two men glimpsed this key: Brian Mulroney of the Progressive Conservatives and Jim Laxer of the New Democratic Party. Mulroney was heeded by his party, Laxer wasn't.

Mulroney and Laxer penetrated the great Canadian political myth: that Canada has a multi-party system with the parties representing differing ideological approaches to government and problem-solving. It must have been more difficult for Mulroney to have perceived this myth than for Laxer. Mulroney was more deeply immersed in the myth since his party had always been considered one of the two major ones. Yet, somehow, Mulroney was able to conclude correctly that Canada is, in fact, a one-party political system.

The only party in Canada, or the only successful one, is the party which *appears* to be successful in the business of regional and cultural conciliation. And, to this can be added two codicils for maintaining Canadian political power: only important regions or cultural groups need to be appeased; and conciliation must be divorced from ideology. Canada is too large and has too many regions with conflicting economic foundations, and too many cultures with differing origins and outlooks, for any one "ideology" to prove acceptable to a majority of the people. Political success in Canada demands that politics of image be substituted for politics of ideology.

Since 1921 the Liberals have been the successful party in Canada and its politics of image was first enunciated, and then refined in action, by Mackenzie King.

All other Canadian parties since 1921, including even the Tories, have only been protest parties motivated by some political, economic or social vision shared only by one Canadian region or culture, or shared at best by two in an uneasy alliance. And, as always, the vision or motivating ideology of the protest parties had proved unpalatable to the other jostling regions and cultures.

The sincerity of the ideology didn't matter, and the possible value of the ideology didn't matter. Canadians have never graduated from regional parochialism to considerations of political philosphy on a national basis.

The *appearance* of the regional and cultural conciliation was all that mattered in the attainment of national political power. As MacKenzie King put it, for example, when trying to woo Western political support: "I want the West to *think* I'm its friend".

King evolved what one writer has called an "ingenious ambiguity" which served to mollify any given region or culture without unduly antagonizing the rest.

King's task took many years and many twists of fate to accomplish, but before he was through he had created the modern Liberal Party, a shifting coalition of as many of the country's interest groups as he could charm, coerce, bribe or otherwise bend to his purposes.[3]

It is absurd to call this kind of outlook a socio-political *ideology* as that term is understood among mature electorates. It is instead a political *technique* for manipulating uninformed, insular electorates.

Brian Mulroney realized that, as a technique, the Liberal Party did not have a monopoly on it and that a similar technique could be adopted by any party of any name... so long as it was prepared to abandon any principle except a determination to remain in power. Appearance of interest-group conciliation was all-important.

Brian Mulroney was uniquely favoured by providence for adopting the politics of image after the Mackenzie King model. Mulroney was as handsome as John Turner, in his own way, but maybe no so pretty. He was young, with an attractive wife, and belonged to the right party at the right time in the right country. All he had to do was bide his time, wait for the inevitable electoral squabble with the Liberals, and ride to power on a protest wave. Only he and his closest advisers had to know that *this* time it would be different. If Brian Mulroney was going to repeat history, it wasn't going to be the depressing history of failure shared by fellow Tories who elected him, instead it would be the successful history of Liberals who had always opposed him. He would become... and by September 4, 1984 *had* become... a determined reincarnation of the founder of the Liberal Party itself, William Lyon Mackenzie King.

This modern instance of spiritual possession has not escaped the notice of some political observers. Assessing Mulroney after six months as Prime Minister, Gerald Kaplan, former NDP federal secretary, wrote in *The Toronto Star* (March 10, 1985):

> It must be acknowledged at once that if an election were held today, the government would repeat its remarkable victory of September, 1984. Since that is precisely the objective of the Prime Minister, it is hardly surprising that he has proved unwilling to move very far beyond public opinion as determined by Allan Gregg of Decima Research. Gregg

replaces the Liberals' polling gury, Martin Goldfarb, and as a result we now have Government by Gregg.

... But governing is about making decisions, often tough decisions which hurt or disappoint someone. Mulroney would rather do neither. So in his unquenchable pursuit of political longevity, he offers, in the glorious tradition of W.L. Mackenzie King, action if necessary but not necessarily action.

Judgements like this one by Kaplan were inspired by Mulroney's own statements, widely reported by Canadian media in March 1985, that his primary objective was simply to remain in power. It was, at least, an honest admission of "ideology" that the Liberals had seldom made in words but had communicated constantly, in action — or non-action.

New Democrats have, in the past, hyped themselves and taunted their opponents with the accusation that there is really no difference between Tories and Liberals, that neither of the "old parties" represented any political philosphy except expediency.

This charge was not only unkind, but untrue. The Progressive Conservative party *has represented* a genuine political philosophy, although it was one in conflict with the ideology of the NDP.

Diefenbaker was genuinely sincere in his vision of Canada, and he made some tough decisions, like the Arrow debacle, which cost him defeat. Perhaps we recall Robert Stanfield's courageous decision, given the fact that Canada did possess a mixed economy of private enterprise and government intervention, of proposing wage and price controls. It was a decision based on a larger view of what Canada needed to halt inflation than mere expediency of party politics... and it cost him an election. And maybe we remember the Liberal campaign policy of pandering to anti-control sentiments before the election and then, after being safely elected, imposing the necessary controls themselves.

And what about Joe Clark? His philosophy was a very real "small-c" conservatism that didn't pretend to be brilliant or glossy, but simply promised relatively small government and relatively honest government. Clark's lonely opposition to Trudeau's unilateral repatriation of the Constitution was a position based firmly on principle rather than political expediency.

It is only since September 1984 that the NDP's accusation has become completely valid. In adopting the governmental *technique* of Mackenzie King, Brian Mulroney *has* transformed the Tories into Grits.

Or, at the very least, Mulroney has served notice that he's committed to the attempt to transform Tories into Grits. Human nature being what it is, since everyone likes success, he will probably succeed. The unprecedented victory of September 1984 will help him. Not compromised by a minority government, and with undisputed majority power and four years to wield it, Mulroney has ample time and opportunity to introduce inexperienced Tories to the heady delights of virtually unlimited corruption, patronage and arrogance. He has time to identify fellow PCs with lingering ideological scruples and to cull them if they cannot be mutated. Since his direction of government and party leadership was not arrived at by the usual process of ideology gradually becoming sold out after tasting power, which is a time-consuming and inefficient way of attaining corruption, but by a conscious determination formed long before September 1984, it is a pretty safe bet that Mulroney will achieve his goal. his goal.

If he does, then he may have created a political configuration even he didn't anticipate. What happens to the other two parties, the Liberals and the NDP?

There's no doubt that Brian Mulroney shrewdly calculated the downward trajectory of Liberal fortunes correctly. Again, the Clark Episode and the Trudeau minority government of 1980 provided the vectors to plot Liberal impact. The aftermath of February 1980 left the Liberals without representation west of Ontario. It became obvious that the Liberals were slowly, surely being reduced to a Quebec regional party. Mulroney completed this geographic checkmate in 1984. And, because of his Baie Comeau origins in Quebec, Mulroney had the unique opportunity, for any modern Tory leader, to actually cut into the Liberal Quebec power base itself.

On the night of September 4, 1984, Mulroney cut into this Liberal power base to the tune of 58 Quebec seats. Mulroney doubtlessly computed the prospects for a Liberal resurgence in 1988 and found them small. The old coalition of Ontario "clear grit" and Quebec *rouges* had, by 1984, long been an anachronism glued weakly together by watery sentimentality and political expedience of power retention. Trudeau's final distinction was unsticking it. Mulroney's talent for non-ideological compromise and conciliation would more likely attract Ontario Liberals into the New Tories... while people with genuine political philosophies, whatever their former political colour, would likely drift toward the NDP.

The NDP.

Although the New Democratic Party between 1961 and 1984 must be considered a failure in terms of a political party whose goal was to attain significant power, the new Canadian political configuration created by Brian Mulroney may have opened up possibilities for the NDP that he did not recognize when he was obsessed with adopting the patina of Liberalism and coping with the persona of John Turner.

Brian Mulroney has not merely usurped the political technique and power of the Liberal Party, and his achievement is not only the destruction of the Liberal Party as a national force. By effectively absorbing the Liberal Party; Mulroney has achieved something much more significant than a partisan victory and the establishment of a new political dynasty. He has created the opportunity for a clarification and polarization of Canadian politics that has not existed since the 1920s and the aftermath of World War I.

It is an opportunity for the NDP to emerge, finally, as a major political party. The question is whether New Democrats can respond to the challenge and can rally the political refugees that Mulroney has scattered into a cohesive force sharing in common a distinctive vision of Canada's future.

* * * * * *

"You know Brian, he's about as ideological as that coffee pot"[4], said Charles McMillan over a room-service breakfast on election day 1984. And McMillan should know. The York University economics professor was Mulroney's chief policy advisor and senior polling augur during the leadership and election campaigns. He knew Mulroney as well as, or better than, anyone and Mulroney trusted him without reservation. "Charley was the only guy whom I allowed to see all our polls"[5], said Mulroney to L. Ian MacDonald, Montreal newsman and biolgrapher-author of *Mulroney, The Making of the Prime Minister.*

The Merriam-Webster Dictionary defines "ideology" as:

1: the body of ideas characteristic of a particular individual, group or culture 2: the assertions, theories and aims that constitute a political, social and economic program

To admit cheerfully that the leader of the Progressive Conservative Party and the Prime Minister of Canada is "as ideological as a coffee pot" is to admit that Brian Mulroney has no ideas that characterize him as an individual and no assertions, theories and aims to constitute any political, social or economic program. It was a curious admission for a policy advisor and polling guru to make, especially since one of Mulroney's biggest problems was combatting the image of being a "plastic man" or "clone" that dogged him in every public opinion sampling since 1976. "The plastic goddamn image was the biggest thing we were fighting"[6], Frank Moores, former Newfoundland Premier and Mulroney campaign aide, recently recalled.

The admission of Mulroney's non-ideology explains how he could, as a nominal Conservative, so easily adopt the political techniques of MacKenzie King's Liberals. For that matter, Mulroney's lack of ideology explains how and why he became a Conservative in the first place. He entered campus politics in 1955 while attending St. Francis Xavier University in Antigonish, Nova Scotia. As he remembered it, the campus Liberals took themselves too seriously since they represented a party that was actually in power, while the Conservatives were "down and out". This is another way of saying that there was less competition for an ambitious young man within the campus PCs than within the campus Liberal establishment. Lack of competition meant a faster and easier road to the top. Within two years, by 1957, Brian Mulroney was leader of the Progressive Conservatives on the St. Francis Xavier campus. By 1961 he was executive vice-president of the national Conservative Students' Federation and one of six young political activists featured in a special issue of *MacLean's* called "The Young Canadians". In his early politics, just as in his later corporate career and his bid for real political power, it was never ideology that motivated Martin Brian Mulroney, but upward mobility... and, like many others of his generation, the emphasis was on the *mobile*, to climb upward as quickly as possible which meant taking the path of least resistance. His choice of party, his chosen career, his political strategy and his government's policies all reflect this mid-1950s North American mindset. Brian Mulroney comes on the Canadian political scene as an honestly self-confessed pragmatist and opportunist with no motivating ideology.

Given Brian Mulroney's life history to date, together with his own statements and those of his closest associates, this would not appear to be an unjust appraisal of Mulroney's basic outlook. Strangely enough, it is not intended to be a critical assessment, either. It has been fashionable to value political leaders who are motivated by ideologies and philosophical principles, or who at least appear to be motivated by them. The assumption is that a foundation of theories and aims will provide a direction for social problem-solving. If there is a preconceived belief about the preferred direction of social evolution, then specific political and economic steps can be devised, based on the guiding ideology, to solve specific problems.

This is a reasonable proposition and has been the reason why democratic electorates have chosen leaders and parties representing fairly well-defined ideologies. But the proposition is reasonable only if the difference between the actual social reality and the desired one is characterized by *problems*. A problem is something that can have one or more *solutions*. It has become so fashionable to talk of problems and "problem-solving" that it is not recognized often enough that some supposed problems are not problems at all, they are really *predicaments*.

A predicament has no *solution*. It can only be responded to in various ways. Ideology is not nearly so helpful in dealing with predicaments as it is in dealing with problems. Ideology can guide the direction of policies intended to be solutions, but predicaments have no solutions.

All nations face both problems and predicaments, but the major difficulty is usually one or the other. Post-war Japan, for example, faced the problem of economic reconstruction for which there were specific solutions. Western Europe faced the same problem after World War II and found similar solutions.

Canada is unique among Western democracies in that its major difficulties are predicaments rather than problems. There are, of course, genuine problems confronting Canadians that can be solved by political and economic decisions. But these problems are a rather minor aspect of the Canadian reality. The major difficulties confronting Canadians are actually predicaments of which specific problems are merely symptoms.

The basic Canadian predicament is the size and nature of the country, and the kind of population distribution dictated by geography and climate. The "bottom line" for colonial settlement was the possibility of mixed farming so that a local population could be self sustaining in basic necessities. Canadian climate and geography conspire to create only four areas suited for mixed farming: Nova Scotia, the St. Lawrence Valley including the north shores of Lakes Ontario and Erie, the Prairies, the Fraser River valley and the Pacific shoreline.

Colonial population concentrated in these four areas where mixed farming could sustain people's basic food requirements and form the basis for secondary economic activities like fishing, mining and manufacture.

But these four areas were widely separated by geography and climate. Between Nova Scotia and the St. Lawrence is the watershed of the Gaspé, the Shick-shock Mountains. Between the St. Lawrence and the Prairies is the rock and muskeg of the precambrian Shield in northern Ontario and Manitoba. Between the Prairies and the Pacific are the Rocky Mountains and the Coast Ranges of British Columbia.

Geography and climate created the basic Canadian predicament of being a country with four separated concentrations of population. History added another predicament to the basic one. The largest mixed farming region, the St. Lawrence Valley, was divided into two regions on the basis of culture and language.

The lower St. Lawrence Valley, from Montreal to the sea, was settled by the French. The upper reaches of the waterway, from

Montreal to the Great Lakes was settled by the English. Where nature had, for once, been generous to Canada by providing a long river road to the continent's heart flanked by land suited to mixed farming because of a rich legacy of glacial silt, the pattern of colonial settlement erected barriers of language and custom in lieu of mountains or muskeg.

Barriers of language and custom created a further Canadian predicament, a political one. Canada inherited the British system of government, a system developed in a densely populated and very small island group. It was a system unsuited for the future development of a North American nation, as the Americans realized when they modified it to better suit continental geography. The British system of government was based on population alone and had no provision for, and no need for, regional representation irrespective of population. But some form of regional representation was necessary within the North American reality of opening up a continent. What was to prevent newly-settled areas from being completely dominated and exploited by older and more densely-populated eastern settlements?

Under the British system, nothing prevented this. The Americans knew that equitable development of the entire continent, the opening up of the west, demanded some governmental institution that protected newly-settled regions from outright domination by older and more established regions. The Americans created their Senate to perform this function. The Senate represented geographic regions, irrespective of size or population, and it allowed emerging western states to fend off economic exploitation by the eastern Establishment.

Canada did not develop a Senate along the American model, a powerful institution suited to the reality of settling an entire continent from east to west. This failure stems directly from the French-English historical predicament in the St. Lawrence Valley. Neither the French nor the English wanted to see new regions with powerful representation. The English feared the power a real Senate might give to French settlers sprinkled all across the country as new territories were established. In the early days of Canada, French-speaking settlers had penetrated wilderness areas from the Atlantic to the Rockies. A Senate on the American model would have been heavily French as new territories gained representation. A Senate on the American model did not appeal to the English colonial masters of a predominantly French-speaking dominion.

The English solution to the problem was to stimulate and encourage immigration of English-speaking colonists, and the American Revolution presented an excellent opportunity to do so. Free land was offered to Loyalists, or to those who professed to have been loyal to Britain during the American Revolution. Once a sufficient number of English-speaking colonists had settled in Canada, sufficient to equal and slightly exceed the French-speaking people in Quebec and elsewhere, the British formed Canada with the British system of government which recognized only population. It was a measure originally intended to ensure continuing English control of Canada, or at least to ensure an English-leaning bias in the balance of power across Canada. And later, a few decades after Confederation, the French realized that times had changed and that an American-style Senate would not work to their advantage. Other regions of Canada had been increasingly settled by English-speakers in the meantime and a geographically-based Senate would reduce Quebec to just one region out of many without giving security to its differing language and culture. The lack of an effective Senate, which first solved a problem for the English and later solved a problem for the French, contributed to another Canadian predicament which causes much political and economic dissatisfaction today.

Canada could not, did not, and has not developed equitably. Central Canada, Ontario and Quebec, with the great majority of population, has controlled and exploited the rest of Canada with the help of the British system of government. Central Canadian manufacturers obtained raw materials from the other regions at very cheap prices and then sold back manufactured goods at inflated prices. Central Canada voted for export restrictions in order to force regions to supply raw material to Ontario and Quebec, and then voted for tariffs to protect the market for the resulting over-priced manufactured goods.

And there is yet another Canadian predicament.

Canada shares the North American continent with the most powerful industrial and military nation in the world. We are anything but completely free to make our own decisions because our economy, and domestic and international policies, are all strongly influenced by the United States.

The Canadian reality is, uniquely among modern Western nations, characterized by predicaments rather than problems. A curious property of predicaments is that sometimes they can be transformed into problems which can then be solved. All that is generally required is a good dose of ideology. The diffilcuty is, however, that the solutions to such transformed problems are often more uncomfortable than the original predicaments.

For example, the French-English predicament could easily be escalated to the status of a problem with the application of a little patriotic ideology on one side or the other, or both. Quebec could separate from, or be expelled from, the Canadian confederation by harsh negotiations or by military confrontation. This *solution* has been proposed by some Quebec nationalists and by some western Canadians, but it is a solution that necessarily involves domestic violence and most Canadians have rejected it for this reason.

As another example, Canada could free itself from American influence and proceed along a social democratic path of political and economic evolution. The predicament of Canadian/U.S. relations could be escalated to the status of a problem by the adoption of social democratic, or even communist, ideology. Then there would be solutions for many problems: Canada could extricate itself from the indignity of being a branch-plant economy by the simple expedient of nationalizing U.S. companies; for a very short time, Canada could pursue its own foreign policy; Canada could achieve, briefly, full employment and boom-time economic growth by developing the large army and military-industrial-complex that would immediately be necessary to cope with the retaliatory U.S. invasion. It is not a solution favoured by most Canadians.

Canada's unique tragedy is that it is beset by predicaments. Some of them, like those dictated by geography and climate, must simply be accepted. But other predicaments, like those born of cultural and political history, can be transformed into problems to be solved . . . but only at grave peril. The solutions to such transformed problems may be worse than the predicaments themselves.

Brian Mulroney is the first Canadian political leader since Mackenzie King to appreciate fully this Canadian reality. Whether he achieved this understanding through conscious analysis or by gut intuition hardly matters, but his biography suggests that he accepted Canadian predicaments as a natural part of his Canadian environment. Brian Mulroney's life has been a response to the various predicaments that, together, define Canada. He is a product of them.

* * * * * *

Brian Mulroney earned his first substantial income singing for an American tycoon. Some critics would say that he's been doing the same thing ever since.

As a boy of seven or eight in Baie Comeau, Brian Mulroney was passionately fond of singing. . .

> Mulroney's first memories were of music, of songs being sung in the kitchen. In his parents' house, there was always a piano, and usually someone plunking away at it. I those pre-television days, family and community singalongs were one of the principal forms of entertainment.
> In this way, Mulroney learned all the old Irish songs and French-Canadian ballads, as well as just about anything that had come down from Tin Pan Alley.[7]

"The Colonel" heard about Brian's singing ability and one day there was a knock on the Mulroney door. Johnny Pope, the company's public relations man, had come to ask if Brian would sing for the boss.

> "Well, Mother said fine, so I remember being driven out there, quite a long drive, by Johnny Pope. And I got up on the piano and they asked him what his favourite song was. And he said that his favourite song was 'Dearie', but that I wouldn't know it, because how could a kid from Baie Comeau be expected to know that.
> But I knew it and I sang it, and others as well. They gave me $50, U.S., and put me in the car and drove me home.

And I gave it to my mother and she just about had a cardiac arrest. Any time he came to Baie Comeau, he'd ask for me and I'd go sing. I'd perform any song that he'd want. He'd just name them and I knew them."[8]

"The Colonel" was Colonel Robert McCormick, owner of the *Chicago Tribune* and the *New York Daily News,* who needed a new supply of pulp and newsprint to feed his presses. In 1936 he began building the mill town of Baie Comeau on the St. Lawrence at the mouth of the Manicouagan and Outardes rivers. Brian's father, Ben Mulroney, saw greater opportunity in the new planned town than in Quebec City and so he moved to Baie Comeau as a member of its pioneer founding generation in 1936. He was a thirty-two year old electrician and married to Mary Irene O'Shea. Brian was born on March 20, 1939.

Brian's performances in singing for The Colonel, who, after all, amounted to something of a feudal lord in Baie Comeau, could conveniently supply a cultural vignette of a Canadian sold out from a young age. A pen-portrait of a born serf, cautious and happy and anxious to please.

But the Canadian predicament is more complex, and more subtle.

Colonel Robert McCormick built anything but a typical mill town at Baie Comeau. He built a model family community complete with hospitals, schools and recreation facilities. He built his town in what has been called an "idyllic setting" over-looking the St. Lawrence river. And although the primary purpose of the new town was, of course, the extraction of pulp and newsprint for McCormick's newspapers, it could not be said that McCormick's town or orientation reflected any ruthless exploitation of either people or the evironment. In fact...rather the opposite. In addition to the mill and the town, McCormick established what amounts to a corporate resort in the wilderness, a "get away" haven called Le Manoir where his American and Canadian executives enjoyed hunting and fishing. McCormick visited Baie Comeau as often as possible, because he loved the land and the sort of community he had created on it. Further, McCormick genuinely appreciated the cultural diversity of his model community with its French Canadian and English Canadian (and American) components.

McCormick's achievement with Baie Comeau stands in ironic contrast to the motivations and achievements of actual Canadians who also possessed sufficient capital to contribute to the country's human and natural resources. These Canadians are, of course, the "Loyalists" of Ontario and Quebec. And they showed scant interest in developing any Canadian region but their own and regarded every planned development and national expansion as an opportunity for exploitation of people and resources. One has only to read of Colonel By's frustration during the canal-building era when eminent Loyalists like Nicholas Sparks indulged in shameless land speculation with the Rideau Canal as the victim. Sparks bought land parcels in the path of the proposed canal, hoping to force the Crown to pay him exorbitant compensation for the resulting necessary expropriation. Never mind that the canal was conceived as a defensive measure for the country and also as a means of opening up settlement of areas further west. Sparks made money on it. His demands were so exorbitant that he forced a detour of the canal, at great expense, through the present city of Ottawa. Sparks Street, in the Nation's capital honours this Loyalist patriot to this day.

Sparks-type civic conceptions were again dominant during the canal-building era when Loyalist businessmen in Montreal and Ottawa made sure that the planned Chambly Canal connecting the St. Lawrence River with Lake Champlain *did not* have the width and depth of the New York State Barge Canal. Natural north-south commerce was, therefore, inhibited to the encouragement of east-west commerce instead. And again, Central Canadian loyalists showed no great inclination to finance a canal from the upper Ottawa River, through Lake Nipissing and along the French River, and into Georgian Bay...a relatively short and significant canal that would have opened up the heart of the continent for Canadians. British North America, in contradistinction to the fledgling United States, possessed natural water-routes into the lakehead, which required only relatively short canalized segments to make these routes useful for western settlement, but the challenge of development was not met by the Loyalists of Central Canada in the 1820s and 1830s.

Instead, the Americans built the much longer Erie Canal in order to connect the Atlantic Coast with the navigable Great

Lakes (above Niagara) and *they* opened up the west first. Indeed, because of American initiative at canal-building, the Americans broke onto the western plains two generations before the Canadians arrived there in any significant numbers. it was this practical American presence, and Canadian *de facto* vacuum, that inspired the mid-19th Century "54' 40" or fight" mentality and the idea of "manifest destiny" that the Americans should control the entire continent. Central Canadian authors and historians are wont to ascribe "manifest destiny" to natural Yankee arrogance, but a more plausible explanation is the failure of their own ancestors to respond to the challenge of opening up a continent because of sheer greed and disinterest, fostered and encouraged by an inadequate system of government.

The failures of the canal-building era, and consequent threat of American annexation of the entire western plains, were exacerbated when railways replaced canalized waterways as arteries of settlement and commerce. Whereas waterways could only be used for about half the year of North America, railways could provide year 'round transport and, consequently a double infusion of people and goods annually onto the western plains. Given the American headstart in populating the west between 1830 and 1850 because of the canals, the newfangled railways provided an even greater threat that the west would be lost to Canada.

Even so, the Loyalists of Central Canada showed scant interest in financing the transcontinental railway without being guaranteed ample land grants along the route and tariff protection for the over-priced manufactured goods that the railroad would carry westward onto the prairies. Large fortunes were made by Canada's Eastern Establishment as the western regions of Canada were developed. One such fortune was the Massey money, obtained by tariff-protected and and over-priced sale of agricultural equipment to hapless prairie farmers. This patriotic fortune is commemorated in Toronto's Massey Hall.

Exploitation of the newly-opened west was not only ruthless, but was even undisguised. It involved a distortion of the British North American Act that few ordinary Canadians are aware of because it is not usually mentioned in school textbooks. Section 103 of the BNA Act guarantees that the resources within a province belong to that province. However, when Alberta and

Saskatchewan were created at the turn of the century, the resources of these two new provinces *belonged to Canada as a whole, not to these two new provinces themselves.* In short, the resources of Alberta and Saskatchewan were open to exploitation by eastern manufacturers with no compensation to the people of these new provinces. It was the start of the tune that is so familiar to us today when, for example, the former Premier of Ontario, Bill Davis, could suggest that Alberta oil should be made available to Ontario below world prices "for the benefit of most Canadians". Ontario mineral resources, however, like nickel, would naturally be sold at the full world price.

The situation was so obvious to western Canadians that, in 1911, an Alberta author named Bramall could write a book entitled *Canada and Her Colonies* which detailed Loyalist/Ontario exploitation of the rest of the country.

It was only by taking their case to the World Court at The Hague that Alberta and Saskatchewan won a decision that returned control of their resources to themselves. The World Court imposed a compensation settlement on Canada's federal government.

For the sake of completeness, it should be mentioned that while the west was exploited, the economy of the Maritimes was destroyed by the east-west trade in Canada and by the imposition of protective tariffs. At the time of Conferation, Nova Scotia was Britain's wealthiest colony. The merchant marine based in the Maritimes was the third largest in the world, after Britain itself and New England. The profits of this carrying trade were immense, and the Maritime economy was healthy in consequence.

It is not generally known to Canadians that Rene Levesque's separatist government in Quebec was not the first separatist government to be elected in a Canadian province. The first separatist government was elected in Nova Scotia immediately after Confederation. Nova Scotia and New Brunswick realized clearly enough that their economies would be destroyed by Confederation.

Maritime fears proved well-founded. By 1920 the enforced pattern of east-west trade and protective tariffs had destroyed the Maritimes' merchant marine economy, and the Atlantic provinces sank into the poverty they exhibit today. But it was not always so. It is still possible to visit the local museum in a small town like Hantsport, Nova Scotia, which boasts an economy solidly based on welfare and unemployment insurance, and at the same time examine the registry of thousands of tons of shipping that used to sail from the little port. No ships sail from there today.

This has not been a digression simply because these aspects of the Canadian predicament were central to Brian Mulroney's formative years in Baie Comeau and his view of The Colonel, Robert McCormick. The bald fact of the matter was that a town like Baie Comeau, created by an American, represented a more humane and equitable development of a Canadian region than anything undertaken by Canadian Loyalists themselves. This was, of course, not something consciously appreciated by the young Brian Mulroney during the early years when he occasionally sang for The Colonel for American money, but it was a realization that must have percolated into his consciousness in later years as an older Brian studied Canadian history and constitutional law.

Brian Mulroney's early experiences in Baie Comeau gave him no reason to fear American people or industry and no reason to fear what might be called "continentalism" with respect to trade, economics and the use of resources.

This outlook, a ready acceptance of the manifold complexities of Canada's predicaments, is reflected in Brian Mulroney's later professional and political career.

After completing his law course in 1964 at Laval University in Quebec City, Mulroney signed aboard Montreal's largest law firm where he worked for ten years. After his first premature bid for the Conservative leadership in 1976, he joined the Iron Ore Company of Canada as a Vice-President, and later as President until he again campaigned for the PC leadership in 1983. Iron Ore Company of Canada was controlled by Hanna Mining of Cleveland, Ohio. In his later professional and business career, just as during his formative years in Baie Comeau, Mulroney apparently saw nothing incongruous about a would-be Canadian political leader working, or singing, for American bosses.

Brian Mulroney's early and later actions were a completely natural and unconscious response to the Canadian predicament-

... completely normal and natural, that is, for a charter member of the "me first" upwardly mobile generation. There's no evidence whatsoever in his life-story that Martin Brian Mulroney was ever so aware of social *problems* that he was inspired to any personal commitment, or sacrifice, to solve them. The ills of society and of his fellow man created no ideology in him other than a personal determination to "make it" and escape those ills himself by taking the path of least resistence always, in perfect conformity with the profile of the Canadian predicament. Mulroney's only apparent goal was to "make it", and "right to the top" — literally. After a decade of success as a corporate lawyer in Montreal, Mulroney was able to buy a substantial pile of bricks "right at the top" of the hill in Westmount, as he once boasted to a friend. It was a suitable residence for an executive of the Iron Ore Company of Canada. Perhaps it reminded Brian Mulroney of the traditional status-by-altitude of mill-town social structure where corporate houses increased with the occupant's importance all the way up to the presidential house on the summit. As L. Ian MacDonald explains it:

> In most company towns, if they didn't have a hill for the management homes, they would build one. In Montreal, some people might regard Mulroney as somewhat *arriviste* for moving to the top of the hill, just as they might sneer at his propensity for wearing Italian loafers. In his own mind, it didn't matter. He had arrived.[9]

Why did a person like Brian Mulroney bother to enter politics? After success as a lawyer and corporate president, did Mulroney have a middle-age identity crisis compelling some sense of social mission?

Not a bit of it.

After receiving media prominence for his part in the Cliche Commission, Mulroney was persuaded by a couple of friends that he had the image to become leader of the Progressive Conservative Party in 1976. His leadership bid, premature as it proved, was not motivated by any vision of what he might be able to achieve as a new Tory leader, or any sacrifice for his country. Instead, his decision became difficult with the simultaneous opportunity to become an executive VP with Iron Ore Company.

But, as a Mulroney cohort, Michael Cogger, put it when recalling how he helped Mulroney decide for the 1976 leadership bid: "There would be other Iron Ores, but the leadership came up only once every ten years." In short, Mulroney conceived of the PC leadership as just another *achievement,* not as an opportunity for serving his country and solving some of its acute problems.

As it turned out, Brian risked nothing but his self-confidence in the 1976 PC leadership convention. He lost out to Joe Clark, but was invited aboard Iron Ore Company anyway. He worked there until his next, and successful, bid for the Tory leadership. Within the context of Mulroney's success orientation, his defeat by Joe Clark in 1976 became, for Brian, a personal *failure*... probably much like a failure to gain a coveted corporate promotion- ... rather than a thwarted attempt to serve his fellow citizens. For some time, Mulroney was personally bitter about the 1976 leadership experience and this was translated into anxiety for his physical health. According to L. Ian MacDonald, he several times feared that he was dying and visited Montreal hospitals to get checked out. According to the same source, Mulroney's drinking increased temporarily. Mulroney's reaction was not typical of those whose commitment has been thwarted, but typical of a balked member of the "me first" junior achievement generation. His 1976 defeat was a personal failure.

Two things are worth noting about a Canadian political leader of this sort.

First, his immense popularity as demonstrated by his September 1984 landslide election is a reflection of the fact that he personifies the values and life-history of most middle-class Canadians of his generation. They, too, have lived life as more or less irrelevant pawns within the Canadian predicament, and their usual response has been to make their lives as comfortable and successful as possible by taking always the path of least resistance.

Second, Mulroney must consider Canadian politics as an irrelevant game. It is important to win, but political leadership and ideology can do nothing to alter the basic Canadian predicament. It is important to win simply because winning is "success", a status thing, not because it provides an opportunity to do anything constructive for the country.

It is easy to see, therefore, how Mulroney could have adopted so easily the convenient morality of W. L. Mackenzie King. And, with so many middle-class Canadians sharing Brian's role within the Canadian predicament, it is easy to see how he was elected so avidly as a vindication of the "sensible" response to the Canadian predicament. It can be said that the existence and election of Martin Brian Mulroney is the symbolic culmination of the Canadian predicament and its effects on Canada's people, an acceptance within the realities of the national parameters. Simply by being, and by getting elected in such a definitive way, Mulroney has spotlighted the Canadian reality for what it is, and has been, and has personalized a particular response to it.

But there are other possible responses, ones which do not consign people to irrelevancy and impotence in a "game" that doesn't really matter anyway.

At least some Canadians, and perhaps a large minority, might well prefer *another* response in 1988. A response, which, for all its pitfalls, might render them something more than pawns in a solution-less predicament.

Does any party carry their banner?

Chapter Three

Tommy Douglas:

Politics of Compassion

The career of Martin Brian Mulroney stands in striking contrast to the life histories of the founders and leaders of the old Co-operative Commonwealth Federation (CCF) and its modern political offspring, the New Democratic Party. The founders of the CCF... J.S. Woodsworth, Major James Coldwell and Thomas Clement Douglas, who became the NDP's first leader ... displayed anything but Mulroney's "successful surrender" to the dictates of Canadian predicaments. These men, the founders of the CCF, were fighters. They recognized Canadian *problems*, and were personally affronted by the human suffering caused by them, and committed themselves to a lifetime of struggle in attempting to alleviate unnecessary human anguish. They were dedicated to improving the world, correcting inequalities and injustices, and their instrument was democratic political action.

Contemporary readers may be excused for assuming that these men must have been dedicated socialists, as that word has come to be defined, and that they were motivated primarily by a belief in Marxist ideology. In fact, many modern NDPers, themselves students of Marxism and neo-Marxism, encourage the automatic assumption that the founders of their party were economic ideologues.

The truth of the matter is rather different. Woodsworth, Coldwell and Tommy Douglas were, in a sense, "anti-Marxists" because they were primarily motivated by what Marx termed derisively "the opiate of the masses" ... religion. Clement Atlee once observed that the British Labour Party "owes more to Methodism than to Marx". Canada's Co-operative Commonwealth Federation, strongly influenced by the developing British Labour Party, likewise owed more to religion than to Marxist dialectics until it was mutated by increasing numbers of urban intellectuals.

The "co-operative commonwealth" that Woodsworth, Coldwell and Douglas envisioned was not inspired by Marxist-style collectivism, but by the Christian ideal of a compassionate community. A favourite heroic verse of Tommy Douglas, which had been adopted as a hymn by the British Labour Party, was taken from Blake's poem, *The New Jerusalem:*

I shall not cease from mortal strife,

Nor shall my sword rest in my hand,
Till we have built Jerusalem
In this green and pleasant land.

This verse, often quoted by Tommy Douglas, was an allusion that puzzled even many loyal CCF voters and which, of course, seemed naive to Marxist-leaning CCF supporters. It is a verse that may have a surprising significance which has escaped conventional political analysis. It is a sentiment which may hold more promise for potential NDP success in the 1988 election than endless debate about modifying Keynesian economics to suit a branch plant economy.

And further, as we come in due course to assess the development of the New Democratic Party under the management of urban, intellectual and Marxist-influenced philosophers like David Lewis, it becomes tempting to conclude that the NDP's marriage to organized labour was a grievous political and social error inspired by outmoded Marxist tunnel vision. Then, I think, one can legitimately question whether successors of Tommy Douglas share his irrepressible and completely natural compassion for humanity. Voters are sometimes more intuitively intelligent than politicians would like to believe. Aloof ideology is not so attractive as human warmth, and it may also be less valid as a problem-solving point of departure. This observation may go part of the way in explaining why Tommy Douglas was able to bring the CCF to power in Saskatchewan, why he was able to win 19 national seats in the NDP's very first federal election... and why the NDP has failed to grow significantly stronger since he stepped down as leader.

* * * * * *

Thomas Clement Douglas was born on October 20, 1904 in Falkirk, Scotland. His father, also named Tom, was a foundry worker. His mother, Annie, had been a factory worker in the Paisley cotton mills. Not unusual for a Scottish working class family of the times, both Tommy senior and Annie placed great emphasis upon education, which meant, under the circumstances, self-education. Annie was fond of poetry and music, the family were frequent borrowers from the library. Young Tommy Douglas ingested great quantities of Robert Burns's poetry, so much, in fact that "Tommy will still quote you Burns at the drop of a hat".

As Tommy himself remembered it, his family were Presbyterians, but their political observances and activities were a good deal more fervent than their religious ones. Falkirk was just going through the process, in company with many other British factory towns, of converting from traditional Liberal loyalties to what would become traditional Labour ones. The political split forming was vehemently argued and even disrupted families. When the elder Thomas Douglas decided to support Labour in the early 1900s, his father (Tommy's grandfather) evicted him from the house ... but later the grandfather, too, switched to Labour and a reconciliation was effected within the family. The young Tommy Douglas was exposed at an early age to political discussion and "political argument was the meat to his meal".

At the age of six, Tommy suffered a minor accident which was later to play a significant part in his political and social outlook. He cut his knee and at first it seemed to be a typical childhood scrape and nothing more, but it failed to heal. Osteomyelitis set in, damaging the lower femur close to the knee.

The Douglas family migrated to Canada in 1910, encouraged by the favourable reports of an uncle, William, who had emigrated earlier. They settled in a rented house on Gladstone Street in Winnipeg's North Side, about eight blocks from the Vulcan Iron Works where Tom senior had landed a job. Nearby was J.S. Woodsworth's All People's Mission, the only community and recreation centre in the district, where Tommy attended a boy's sports program ... or, at least, attending as best he could in view of his bad leg. He was frequently on crutches and, during the winter before an unexpected and successful operation, he was carried to school aboard a sled voluntarily pulled by two immigrant boys, whom he barely knew. They spoke little English and could not really converse with Tommy and, in his later years, Douglas would wonder what motivated them to these acts of kindness. Their compassion was one small bit of evidence that bred a deep ultimate faith in humanity in T.C. Douglas.
humanity in T.C. Douglas.

But the bad leg could not be ignored, the osteomyelitis was getting worse. In the hospital for a "final" operation, Tommy was a ward patient and entitled only to routine attention by the physicians on duty. His family could not afford any specialist's assessment of the problem. He was informed that his leg would have to be amputated. By chance, however, a prominent Winnipeg orthopaedic surgeon, Dr. R.H. Smith, visited Tommy's ward along with a group of his medical students. Tommy's leg interested him and Dr. Smith thought that the case would provide valuable instruction for the students. Accordingly, Dr. Smith obtained permission to try an operation that might save the leg. Smith was successful, although he at first feared that Tommy's knee would never bend. By efforts of will, Tommy did manage to bend the knee, and to exercise it, so that he was later able to hike, play soccer and even to win amateur boxing tournaments.

However, his "luck" affected Tommy Douglas deeply. . .

My father had no coverage for accidents or medical needs. There was no workman's compensation, and there was nothing for the families of the poor. To go to an orthopaedic surgeon was, for us, simply out of the question. And if my father had been seriously disabled in his work by the molten metal which did, several times, burn him severely, there would have been no money to take care of my mother, my sister or myself.

When I thought about it, I realized that the same kind of service I got by a stroke of luck should have been available to every child in that ward, and not just to a case that looked like a good specimen for exhibition to medical students.[1]

"The Medicare program of Saskatchewan when Tommy was Premier came directly from the fear of a poor boy that he would lose his leg, and a sense of the unfair caprice that saved it for him."[2]

The Douglases returned to Scotland when war broke out in 1914 because Thomas senior felt duty-bound to enlist. While Thomas served in the army, the Douglas family lived with Annie's parents, the Clements, in Glasgow. Annie sold sewing machines, and Tommy took odd jobs, in order to supplement the

$1.00 per day that was allowed the family on Thomas senior's soldier's salary.

In order to pay his way with his school's fees in Glasgow, Tommy worked as a "whisker-soaper" for a local barber at 6 shillings per week. This money went to sustain the family and Tommy soon found a way to augment it. In his spare time he made a decorative wooden box suitable for holding coinage, and he inscribed it "For the Boy" and made sure it was placed near the cash register. He was soon receiving, in tips, more than his salary. During the Christmas season, and other festive occasions, he'd make £2 per week. Since there were as many festive occasions as the sailors of Glasgow chose to create. Tommy made a good wage in wartime Glasgow.

During the summer of 1918 Canada very nearly lost a future political leader to the call of commercial adventure and romanticism. Young Tommy got a job in a cork factory in Glasgow owned by a Mr. Hunter and made a very favourable impression because of his quick intelligence and capacity for hard work. Tommy was rapidly promoted from the factory floor to the office and Hunter, who had no sons of his own, wanted to pay Tommy's way to night school where he could learn Portuguese and Spanish. It was Hunter's plan to send him off on voyages as a buyer of cork. Since his two transatlantic voyages had made a powerful impression on Tommy, so much so that he wanted to become a sailor, Hunter's plans were a powerful, and flattering, attraction to him. Tommy was also earning £2, 10s, per week, or more than Thomas senior ever earned as a foundry worker.

Luckily for the landlocked province of Saskatchewan, Thomas returned from the European fighting before Hunter's schemes could mature and the Douglas family set sail across the Atlantic for a third time on January 1, 1919 to move to Canada and Winnipeg.

Thomas again found work at the Vulcan Iron Works, Tommy got a job as an apprentice in the printing trade with Richardson Press which produced the *Grain Trade News,* and the family rented a house on Gordon Street near their old neighborhood.

Tommy arrived back in Winnipeg just in time to witness the build-up and culmination of the Winnipeg General Strike. This strike was one small symptom of wide-spread disillusionment that gripped the entire Western world after World War I. It was a disillusionment so profound that it stimulated a significant shift in politics and social orientation during the post-war decades in both North America and in Europe. Millions of working class people had naively and patriotically marched off to World War I because their social and political leaders had appealed to their national loyalty. After four years of brutal carnage, these same working class people returned home to economies characterized by soaring inflation and few available jobs. For a significant minority of these people, naivety had been burned away by battlefield experiences and by trench-education supplied by socialists. Why were working people in pre-war Europe consigned to poverty when, magically, huge sums were found to conduct the war? When soldiers, like Thomas Douglas, were fighting for pay of $1.10 per day and their families were consequently living in desperate circumstances as the price of this patriotism, why were the "captains of industry" allowed to make huge war profits on human suffering? Why, in short, was society organized for the benefit of a very few who profited in war and peace alike from the sacrifices of the great majority?

The conviction grew in these returning veterans that society could be organized for the benefit of greater numbers of people. It was a realization that eventually brought the Labour Party to power in Britain, that eventually brought the CCF to power in Saskatchewan, that supported the "New Deal" of FDR in the United States. It was the same disillusionment and re-assessment of society that motivates the NDP presently in Canada and which inspired the New Left during the American 1960s. It was the realization of a choice between a society run for the benefit of a relatively small group of "capitalists" whose economic system depends heavily upon periodic wars and armaments production, or for a society organized for the benefit of the greater majority of humanity which has little investment in industrial ownership.

That, over-simplified, was the choice compelled by post-World War I realizations among returning veterans and their families in 1919 ... and that, over-simplified, remains the choice today.

Again, over-simplified, there were two main streams of social philosophy sharing this realization and sharing a determination to change society.

One stream could be called "religious" in that its proponents were motivated primarily by a desire to exchange war-prone capitalism for a social community based on Christian, or human compassion. Capitalism, for this group, was not an estate or a class, but simply a manifestation of human avarice ... free enterprise carried to the point of harming others was, simply, sinful. It was un-Christian, it was a betrayal of human responsibility and promise.

The other stream of dissent was Marxism, which saw the problem in a somewhat different light. Born of 19th Century materialist science, Marxism placed little faith in "religion" or "spirituality" as a trustworthy mechanism for promoting a change of history and society. Marxism was another development of 19th Century science which rejected religious explanations for man's development, man's history and man's social structure. Just as Darwin had challenged the religious account of humanity's creation and development, so Marxism challenged the religious view of humanity's creation and development. It is no accident that Marx originally wanted to dedicate *Das Capital* to Darwin. Marxism claimed a scientific explanation for the pattern of history and a scientific methodology for promoting social evolution. Marxism saw all of history as a mechanistic conflict between the producers of wealth, the workers, and the owners of wealth, the capitalists. For the Marxists, the solution for society was simple: producers had to become also the owners of wealth. Marxism viewed human history as the long, but inevitable process of producers taking over the ownership of wealth as they became educated and organized. Marxists viewed mankind as an economic animal, not one motivated by spirit or divinity, and saw history as a mechanical process of workers gaining ownership of wealth they created ... not as a struggle to attain a more God-like state of grace.

Within the Marxist camp itself there were two main streams of thought. The "communists" believed that the capitalist owners of wealth would never give up their privileges voluntarily or by democratic process, and that the workers would have to rebel violently to take over the ownership of wealth they created. The "socialists", on the other hand, believed that a transfer of wealth ownership from Capitalists to actual producers of wealth could be achieved through democratic processes.

The religionaries and the Marxists alike appreciated the very real social problems that characterized the post-World War I Western world, but they saw the problem in different ways. Yet, their differing viewpoints had enough in common to create an alliance of sorts which persists to this day . . . but with misgivings on both sides.

Those religious functionaries who were committed to the achievement of a Jerusalem on earth by combatting unconscionable avarice were wary of the Marxists' essentially mechanical and unhuman view of mankind. For their part, the Marxists harboured the most profound suspicions of religion, knowing well enough that organized religion had always, when the chips were down, supported the capitalists and the war economy that kept them in social control. The "God is on our side" message, preached from establishment churches" pulpits, had always sent common people off to fight for the benefit of a very few at the top of the economic pyramid.

Nonetheless, in spite of their mutual misgivings, an alliance between socialist Marxists and "dissenting" ministers was possible, and it was forged . . . these dissenting religious leaders being Baptists, Methodists, Presbyterians and others who were not establishment Church of England or Roman Catholic. It was, in a way, the strangest of political and social alliances, and it remains so. It is an essential contradiction within political parties like the CCF and the modern NDP.

This strange alliance is what Clement Atlee meant when he said that the British Labour Party owed more to Methodism than to Marx. Many of the most prominent British labour leaders came from the religious stream of the alliance not from the Marxist, and the same thing happened in Canada with the CCF. Many of the CCF's prominent founding personalities came from the "old country" with Labour Party *and* religious affiliation.

It is interesting that the essential contradiction between Marxism and "dissenting" Christianity within the CCF and the NDP was, and is, dramatically and personally illustrated by two powerful personalities. Tommy Douglas represented the Christian-motivated component, while David Lewis represented the Marxist parentage.

Religion of all sorts, whether "dissenting" or "establishment", has suffered a decline in significance and prestige over the past 30-40 years, but especially since the wrenching experience of the Second World War. The religious component of the social democratic alliance has, therefore, suffered a decline of significance, prestige and credibility in the modern world. The Marxist view has seemed more "scientific" and "relevant" to socialist politics since about 1960 and, naturally, *economics* has been the primary focus of socialist parties like the NDP. This has been a natural evolution and one stimulated by the coincidental crisis of North America's industrial and energy situation.

However, in spite of its apparently logical claim to a "scientific" foundation, it may be that Marxism is a flawed lens when it comes to viewing the "truth" about man's progress as compared to the lens offered by dissenting religion. This is a possibility suggested not by wistful spirituality or by fanatical personal belief, but simply by hard facts. If so, this indicates that Canada's social democratic party, the NDP, might escape its present stagnation by widening the definition of "social" beyond Marxist economics and address itself to a more visionary conception of human society. It may be that the outlook of T.C. Douglas was always more "scientific" (in terms of being based on *fact*) than the perspective of David Lewis, and that the electorate sensed this, which explains the success of Tommy Douglas and the stagnation of the NDP under the Eastern ideologues and organizers.

In 1919, during the summer of the Winnipeg Strike, young Tommy Douglas witnessed this outburst of profound disillusionment among common people under the leadership of personalities who included both "Methodists" and "Marxists".

The strike actually started on May 15 with a walkout of construction and metal trades employees, but support spread among other workers until the city was almost completely paralysed. At first the strikers themselves maintained the peace and took the advice of the *Daily Strike Bulletin:* "just eat, sleep, play, love, laugh and look at the sun." But a large number of angry and disillusioned veterans joined the strikers' cause, because of maturing sentiments already discussed, and it was these people who first took to the streets in parades and demonstrations. Then, Marxist activists exploited the situation with dogmatic rhetoric about a basic upheaval of society and getting power and wealth into the hands of the producers. The Bolshevik "October Revolution" was fresh in the minds of the Conservative government in Ottawa, the fiery speeches of some union organizers therefore had a sinister ring, and everyone was dismayed by the size and vehemence of the street demonstrations. It seemed that the *status quo* might indeed be overturned in Winnipeg...at least, it seemed that way to the professional and business people of the city. They formed the Citizens Committee of One Thousand, encouraged the formation of anti-strike groups and recruited squads of "special police" to uphold law and order as they saw it.

It was inevitable that the strikers and anti-strikers would clash, and they did. On June 10, 1919 a minor riot broke out. It was enough to frighten Arthur Meighen's government into over-reaction. Ottawa quickly passed amendments to the Immigration Act and the Criminal Code to permit deportation of the British-born organizers of the strike, and Ottawa rushed Mounties and heavy armaments to Winnipeg. And, naturally, the Eastern papers indulged in that brand of journalism all too familiar in Canada where, for sheer titillation the conflict was over-blown into deliciously dangerous proportions. The Eastern press screamed that the strikers were Reds and it was easy to believe (from newspaper accounts, at any rate) that a Bolshevik-style revolution was being unleashed from Winnipeg, and might spread to engulf the rest of the country. No one asked whether this was plausible or even possible. Hysteria gripped the Eastern establishment. Arthur Meighen pronounced: the "so-called strike was a cloak for an effort to overturn proper authority".

Things came to a head on June 21 with exciting events. The Mounties armed with clubs and guns charged into a crowd of strikers. A streetcar was overturned, if not the government, two people were killed and many were injured. Many were also arrested during this period of confrontation.

Fred Dixon, publisher of *Western Labour News,* was arrested and turned over management of the paper to J.S. Woodsworth, a Methodist minister and head of the All People's Mission which Tommy had visited during the family's previous residence in

Winnipeg. But Woodsworth was arrested just two days after Dixon on charges of sedition for publishing the following:

> And they shall build houses, and inhabit them: and they shall plant vinyards, and eat the fruit of them. They shall not build, and another inhabit; they shall not plant and another eat; for as the days of a tree are the days of my people, and mine elect shall long enjoy the work of their hands.

As government prosecutors subsequently discovered, this "seditious libel" was a passage from the Bible, from Isaiah. Further, as investigation revealed: "police raids across Canada-...found no evidence of an attempt to arm any branch of the workers movement". The government's heavy-handed action had the opposite of its intended effect because public sympathy came heavily down for the strikers. Most of those arrested were released from jail within a year or less, and more than a few "were promptly elected to city government, the provincial legislature, and the House of Commons".[3]

By chance, on that 21st of June, young Tommy Douglas had been delivering the *Grain Trade News* to offices in the Grain Exchange building when the final riot began. He and a friend climbed a pole to reach a vantage point atop a two storey building and saw the whole confrontation between Mounties and strikers.

The events of the day deeply affected Tommy Douglas in at least two ways. First, the presence of the many veterans in the riot made him appreciate the depth of anger and dissatisfaction caused by a post-war economic slump, the hatred and futility men felt for fighting in defence of a system that did not offer economic or social justice to themselves and their families. It was a lesson he kept firmly in mind a quarter of a century later when he led the CCF to power in Saskatchewan in the election of 1944. Douglas became committed to breaking the "boom and bust" cycle of capitalist military-industrial economics. Second, at some point Douglas grew wary of government's tendency to curtail civil liberties because of *supposed* grave threats to national security. This wariness manifested itself 51 years later when Douglas led the NDP in lonely opposition to Trudeau's imposition of the War Measures Act because of the so-called "Quebec Crisis" of 1970.

The Winnipeg General Strike of 1919 and the "Quebec Crisis" of 1970 had a great deal in common. Both situations were blown entirely out of proportion by the Eastern media, and completely unjustifiable panic was promoted by government and media alike. Also, in both cases, the brunt of the over-response was borne by a region of Canada other than the headquarters of the Eastern Establishment, Ontario.

But, as in the case of the Winnipeg situation where subsequent investigation "found no evidence of an attempt to arm any branch of the workers movement", the same held true in the aftermath of the "Quebec Crisis" where a police search of revolutionary weapons throughout the entire province turned up only a few firearms "that could be found any time in a little city like Nanaimo"[5]. The British Diplomat, James Cross, whose abduction by the "revolutionaries" started the whole crisis, said later he was kidnapped by "six kids trying to start a revolution". So much for the revolutions of 1919 and 1970. Charitably, they were figments of governmental over-reaction. Less charitably and more plausibly, they were political hoaxes perpetrated by Arthur Meighen in 1919 and by Pierre Elliot Trudeau in 1970 to serve their own political ends. Meighen and the Eastern Establishment wanted an excuse to nip any socialist movement in the bud. Trudeau and the Eastern Establishment wanted an excuse to nip separatism in the bud.

It is very probable that Tommy Douglas's personal experience of the Winnipeg General Strike gave him the insight to doubt Trudeau's justification for imposing the War Measures Act in 1970. Douglas, alone among political leaders during the "Quebec Crisis" did not jump on the bandwagon of over-reaction. At the time, Douglas and the NDP were criticized for their refusal to support Trudeau. But later, as the paltry facts of the Quebec rebellion came to light, even Robert Stanfield, PC leader who did support the imposition of the War Measures Act, came to regret his lack of judgement during the days of October 1970 when he supported Trudeau under highly emotional pressure from his party.

It is interesting to note here that the over-reaction of Trudeau in 1970 had the same effect as Meighen's heavy-handedness in 1919. Meighen wanted to derail any socialist movement before it could get started, but succeeded only in making martyrs of the strikers so that a strong socialist movement did emerge on the prairies. Trudeau wanted to awe the separatist movement with a show of force. Almost all of the Parti Quebecois organizers were rounded up under the War Measures Act in spite of the fact that they worked for a legally recognized political party whose leader, Rene Levesque, had denounced the FLQ as "madmen". Far from intimidating Rene Levesque and the PQ, Trudeau's tactics brought them to power in Quebec.

Very possibly it was the Winnipeg General Strike that bred in youthful Tommy Douglas a scrupulous respect for civil liberties and a high tolerance for conflicting points of view. Among other things, he must have perceived that lack of respect for civil liberties, and lack of tolerance for diversity, aside from being unjustifiable in a human sense, often had a tendency to backfire on authority in both politics and society. Meighen was largely responsible for bringing into being the very thing he feared, a viable socialist movement in the west. Tommy Douglas, early on, must have made a vow to avoid similar mistakes out of short-sighted and misguided intolerance. When, late in his career, the NDP was "threatened" by the influence of Waffle radicals, it was old-fashioned Tommy Douglas who saw nothing particularly frightening about them, and it was "modern" David Lewis who purged them from the party with the justification of maintaining an ideological purity. Ironically, the very recent (1983) criticisms of James Laxer, a former Waffler who left the NDP under pressure, point out the growing irrelevancy of the NDP as David Lewis structured it and molded it for his successor, Ed Broadbent.

Perhaps it was this realization of the needs for tolerance that led Tommy Douglas to adopt the religious/humanitarian approach toward promoting social change rather than to adopt the more dogmatic Marxist/economic orientation toward social evolution.

* * * * * *

But another factor in Douglas's decision to become a minister was the Masons and the Order of De Molay.

Like many Scottish working class parents, the elder Thomas Douglas held education in great respect, both for its own sake and for the better life it could guarantee in a purely material sense. He had been upset when Tommy immediately went to work, at age 14, when the family returned to Winnipeg after World War I. But the realities of the Douglas family finances simply didn't permit Tommy to go to school. Tommy promised to return to his education when the family achieved some financial security, and in the meantime he worked hard in the printing shop. He became a linotype operator at the age of 16 and received a journeyman's wage before his five years of apprenticeship were completed.

In the years between 1919 and 1924 the Masons and their junior Order of De Molay played an important part in his life, and it was during these years that he decided to become a minister. A prominent Winnipeg Mason, W.J. Major, later Attorney-General of Manitoba, was instrumental in causing Tommy to decide for the ministry.

Like many contemporary people, Doris French Shackleton, a biographer who worked closely with Douglas in order to write an account of his life, doesn't quite know what to do with Tommy's exposure to the Masons and the Order of De Molay. In company with many others, Shackleton didn't take these Masonic years very seriously even though they were instrumental in forming Tommy Douglas's later career and commitment. In her biography, *Tommy Douglas,* she does not regard the Masons as a religion, but as something of a social club on the order of the Boy Scouts. She writes:

> Annie Douglas was the religious influence in the home and it was she who took most pride in Tommy's growing interest in the church. His father had become cynical of the Christian offices performed by chaplains at the fighting front. He donated money to the Salvation Army, and stayed away from the church.
>
> The earliest occasion Douglas speaks of, when his platform skill evoked a profound audience response, involved a sympathetic moment shared by father and son. Tom Douglas had shown an interest in the Masonic Order, but it was Tommy who involved himself deeply in the junior Order of De Molay. This youth organization had spread widely

through the United States after the First World War. A chapter was formed in Winnipeg. One of its high moments was a dramatic production before a convention of Masons held in the old Board of Trade building at the corner of Portage and Main. The play concerned the life and death of the patron of the junior order, Jacques De Molay, the fourteenth century knight-at-arms who led expeditions against the Saracens, and was put to death as a heretic by Philip the Fair of France. Tommy took the title role and threw himself heroically into the part. He spoke of that evening:

> "My father was there and he was sparing of praise as in most things. When we came out he said, 'Let's walk' which we did, for a distance of about four miles. I knew he had been deeply moved. There was never a word. We walked in silence. Going up the front steps he tapped me on the shoulder and said, 'you did no bad.'"[6]

Later, Shackleton writes about Tommy's decision to enter the ministry:

> Douglas is reluctant to talk about experiencing a "call". He is more apt to joke about impromptu prayers at De Molay meetings. . .[7]

The years between 1919 and 1924, are the years in which Tommy Douglas decided the future course of his life, and yet there is very little information available about this period. These were years spent contemplating the ministry — years learning about and being influenced by Masonic ideals. This is an important chapter in Tommy Douglas's life, a period when he formulated his future commitment to the betterment of mankind through social and political action. It is a story which I think, has great possible relevance to the future of Canada and the NDP.

Having decided to enter the ministry, Tommy began a 6-year matriculation course at Brandon College which, at that time, was affiliated with McMaster University. He financed his schooling by doing weekend supply preaching for smaller churches that could only afford a student minister.

In his third year at Brandon College, Douglas met Stanley

Knowles who had just come up from Los Angeles. They shared the academic medals between them in friendly competition. Tommy maintained that he "tried to take the gold medals, but they made me put them back."[8] Knowles admitted that "Tommy was smarter, but I was better at writing exams."[9] Both Knowles and Douglas preached, on alternate Sundays, at The Calvary Baptist Church in Weyburn, Saskatchewan through the winter of 1929-1930. With the approach of ordination in June, 1930, the congregation at Weyburn had to decide between Douglas and Knowles in a secret vote. Douglas won narrowly, and Knowles went to the First Baptist Church in Winnipeg.

Douglas gained more than a congregation in June 1930. While sometime "supply preaching" at Carberry Presbyterian Church, Tommy met Irma Dempsey, the daughter of a local farmer. She had originally been Methodist, but transferred to the Presbyterian church in order to hear him preach. Later, she contrived to study music at Brandon College "and wound up her course, whether by accident or good timing, the same year that Tommy graduated with distinction and moved on to his first charge". Douglas quipped in later years: "Of course they used to warn the girls at college to stay away from the theologs, or they'd end up in a drafty manse somewhere, getting their clothes out of a missionary box."[10] Although that is precisely what happened to Irma over a number of years, the prospects never daunted her. Tommy and Irma were married in the summer of 1930.

Martin Brian Mulroney and Thomas Clement Douglas began their respective careers at about the same age, but, of course, their respective choices were in stark contrast. While Mulroney headed for corporate law after graduation, Douglas looked forward to a poverty-stricken ministry on the prairies. And the "Dirty Thirties" were just starting in Saskatchewan although things had been bad for some time. Douglas made his choices to help people, Mulroney made his to help himself. What did Douglas intend to preach about in Weyburn?

> Oh you always start with a (Biblical) text. But the Bible is like a bull fiddle, you can play almost any tune you want on it. My background, being interested in social and economic questions, naturally inclined me to preaching the idea that religion in essence was entering into a new relationship with

God and into a new relationship with the universe. And into a new relationship with your fellow man. And that if Christianity meant anything at all, it meant building the brotherhood of man. If you really believed in the fatherhood of God, if you believed what Jesus said, that we live in friendly universe, then the brotherhood of man was a corollary to it. And that meant a helpful relationship between man and man, building a society and building institutions that would uplift a society and building institutions that would uplift mankind, and particularly those who were the least fortunate, and this was pretty well the sort of message I was trying to get across.[11]

It was the sort of message that got across. From the unlikely career start in Weyburn, T.C. Douglas went on to help M.J. Coldwell and J.S. Woodsworth to found the Co-operative Commonwealth Federation, become the 4-term Premier of Saskatchewan and introduce many of the social programs that Canadians take for granted today — programs that other-party federal governments in Ottawa were forced to adopt under pressure, and become the first leader of the New Democratic Party. It was not an easy road, nor an obvious one the first time he played the bull fiddle in Weyburn.

The thirties *were* really dirty in Saskatchewan. Not only did the world-wide Depression reduce prices for everything, but Saskatchewan experienced years of drought. The soil dried up and blew away, and the land that once produced 16 bushels of wheat per acre then produced only 3. In some areas of Saskatchewan 90 per cent of the population had no income. It was into this social situation that Douglas came as a young minister with "socialist" tendencies.

At that time I thought, "well, something's got to be done." I didn't think in terms of politics. I thought in terms of the church making some pronouncements on social and economic conditions. Setting forth some sort of goals for a better type of society. That was as far as my mind went. I could do practical things.[12]

He and Irma began to organize the unemployed, setting up an odd-job agency providing labour at 25¢ an hour. Their home became a community recreation and organization centre in an

effort to keep disgruntled and desperate young people out of
trouble. The youngsters gathered to converse and to produce
plays for mutual distraction. Douglas collected money to pay
freight charges on fruit and vegetables from British Columbia
which were substandard (or slightly spoiled) and scheduled for
dumping. "The young men sorted the produce into bags at Weyburn station, and poeple came with baskets or wheelbarrows to
take it home".

The church basement became an emporium for clothing and
bedding contributed by Baptist churches in Ontario and Quebec
...and Douglas himself became a "nuissance".

> I had a lawyer in my congregation. One morning I dropped
> in at his office and he took issue with me about having any
> part in this unemployment association. I said he only saw
> affluent clients, people concerned with the purchase and
> sale of real estate and so on. Had he ever seen the poorer
> part of the city? He said he'd lived in Weyburn twenty-five
> years. But I took him to homes that had hardly any coal, the
> children had no clothes to go to school and hadn't had milk
> for a week. I took him to talk to the school nurse. He said he
> wouldn't have believed it. Weyburn had the highest relief
> schedules in the province but it didn't meet the need.
>
> I learned a very hard lesson. You have to take a stand.
> Either with the sheep or with the fellow who's shearing
> them. The moment you take a stand with the unemployed
> you're in trouble with the taxpayers who say, "If they get
> more I get less". So the logical thing for preachers is to get
> back to generalities. "We must all love each other. If there
> was more love, and if everybody was honest and decent, we
> wouldn't have any of these troubles".
>
> I was becoming labelled as a dangerous radical in the
> community, stirring up the unemployed to ask for more
> money and sticking my nose in places that were none of my
> business. I had several bad set-to's with provincial relief
> officers who would come down to tell the city council they
> were spending too much money, they had to make cuts. And
> I would go before them with these cases of children needing
> milk and clothing and the school nurse's report. I was a
> nuisance.[13]

He became more of a nuisance in September 1931, during the
infamous Estevan strike and riot. The workers had organized a

union against opposition from local coal mine owners and on September 8 the union struck for better wages and working conditions. The miners had been making 37½ cents an hour, but the owners reduced this to 32½ cents an hour. Before the drought the miners had accepted this meagre income meekly, partly because they could augment it by doing agricultural work during the summer. But with the drought, the opportunities for extra agricultural work decreased sharply. In 1931, the miners were paid by the weight of the coal they brought to the surface, but were being cheated on the weighing process by the company.

To make matters worse, the miners were forced to buy from the company store which, naturally, charged higher prices than other stores in Estevan. The miners and their families lived in shacks and remained in hopeless debt to the company store.

The miners struck to improve their lot. The Douglases travelled to Estevan, just a little south of Weyburn, to see the situation first-hand. Irma, particularly, was appalled by the living conditions of the mining families. Douglas not only preached against the unfair situation from his pulpit, but his congregation in Weyburn donated a truckload of food to send to the strikers of Estevan.

Inevitably, communists and doctrinaire Marxists, then got into the act with a performance that Tommy Douglas was never able to forget. Professional organizers came from Saskatoon to help the miners, claiming that they had the support of the "Red International of Soviet Russia". This thoroughly alarmed the mine owners and the government, and the former were able to convince the latter to send a special squad to Esteven. The town council passed a bylaw prohibiting demonstrations. Unfortunately, the miners were not informed of this bylaw when a supporting contingent from Bienfait arrived by cavalcade and attempted to reach the mines by driving down the main street of Estevan. This cavalcade clashed with police, there was a riot, the police fired into the crowd killing three men.

A monument was later erected in Bienfait's cemetery over the graves of the victims and inscribed; "murdered in Estevan Sept. 29, 1931 by RCMP".[14]

Douglas was labelled a "Red" for his association with the miners even though he had nothing but contempt for the way the miners had been led into a confrontation by the communist agitators. His concern had been with improving the miners' welfare, not with preparing any ground for a communist revolution.

In addition to the donated truckload of food, Douglas had managed to get some food, clothing and monetary support for the Estevan miners from the United Farmers organization and from the Independent Labour Party. After the strike he realized that piecemeal action on a "per strike" or "per crisis" basis would not solve the underlying problems for either farmers or workers. He wrote to J.S. Woodsworth who, by that time, had become a Labour M.P. from Winnipeg. Perhaps groups like the United Farmers and the independent Labour Party could be combined into a larger organization that could more effectively lobby government for the necessary relief measures, or even begin to field candidates in elections on a socialist and Christian platform.

By chance, Woodsworth thad just received a somewhat similar suggestion in a letter from M.J. Coldwell, a Regina Alderman who was on the Relief Committee of the municipality. In letters to both Coldwell and Douglas, Woodsworth suggested that the two men should get together and discuss what could be done. The Saturday after receiving his letter from Woodsworth, Coldwell drove to Weyburn to meet Tommy Douglas. This meeting was, effectively, the birth of the Co-operative Commonwealth Federation, or CCF. The party was formed in the minds of three men: J.S. Woodsworth, a former Methodist minister; M.J. Coldwell, a Devon-born teacher steeped in British Labour Party philosophy; and Tommy Douglas, a Baptist preacher. As with the British Labour Party, Canada's CCF owed more to religion than the Marxism in its early formative stages.

Woodsworth was federal leader of the CCF until succeeded by Coldwell who led the party up to the time of its metamorphosis into the NDP in 1961. Tommy Douglas became the first leader of the NDP because he had brought the first socialist government in North America to power in Saskatchewan. The development of the NDP from the CCF can be followed more conveniently by a focus on Douglas.

The basic idea of CCF came directly from Douglas's practical experience in trying to help the Estevan miners ... there had to be a co-operative coalition of farmers and labour on the prairies instead of a multiplicity of unconnected farm and labour groups who acted in an uncoordinated manner on a "per crisis" basis.

During 1932 people like Coldwell, Woodsworth, Douglas, Clarence Fines and George Latham, as well as many others, worked to set up a major convention for 1933 based on the participation of the many farm and labour organizations that existed independently on the prairies, along with 45 farm/labour delegates recruited from Ontario to make up the appearance of a national party. The actual founding convention of the CCF took place in Regina during July 19-21, 1933. An eight-point social platform for the new party was drawn up by a committee of three westerners (M.J. Coldwell, Robert Gardiner and George Latham) which was subsequently drafted into stirring socialist language by Professor Frank Underhill and which became known as the "Regina Manifesto". The eight points were:

1. The establishment of a planned system of economy for the production, distribution and exchange of all goods and services.

2. Socialization of the banking, credit and financial system of the country together with the social ownership, development, operation and control of utilities and natural resources.

3. Security of tenure of the worker and farmer in his home.

4. Retention and extension of all existing social legislation and facilities with adequate provision for insurance against crop failure, illness, accident, old age and unemployment.

5. Equal economic and social opportunity without regard to sex, nationality or religion.

6. The ecouragement of all co-operative enterprises which are steps toward the achievement of the co-operative commonwealth.

7. Socialization of health services.

8. The federal government should accept responsibility for

the unemployed and supply suitable work or adequate maintenance.[15]

As David Lewis was later to observe in his memoirs published in the 1980s, taken literally the Manifesto left precious little room for "free enterprise" of any sort and, further, some of Underhill's "stirring" socialist language had been incorporated to appease what Lewis called "hard-line Marxists". It was rousing stuff to the prairie socialists of the time, and scary stuff for both eastern and western "free enterprises" alike. Naturally enough, when the CCF looked very likely to come to power in Saskatchewan (which they did) and in Ontario (which they did not) some 11 years later, the "Regina Manifesto" gave sufficient cause for political opponents to predict the imminent end of the existing social order. And, needless to say, when the CCF *did* come to power in Saskatchewan, the literal interpretation of the Manifesto was quietly ignored in favour of the "spirit" of it. Freedom and free enterprise remained alive and well in Saskatchewan under Tommy Douglas... and the only party which threatened political liberty was the Liberals which postponed the legally-required election for a year under the excuse of a "war measure" in the hopes of campaining sufficiently to defeat the CCF. This war measure, like the one in 1970, backfired in its intent.

Yet, for all that, The "Regina Manifesto" was a remarkable Canadian political document, revealing the depth of dissatisfaction on the prairies — the depth of despair.

In the Saskatchewan provincial election of 1934 Douglas unhappily followed the campaigning advice of his ex-teacher political mentor, Coldwell, who maintained that it was necessary to communicate with the peoples' intellect and not to pander to their emotions. Coldwell's political speeches were more like economics lectures. It is a measure of the interest and education of the Saskatchewan rural electorate that Coldwell's educational and academic approach, while not *always* successful, actually got him elected regularly. In 1934, however, with the CCF barely launched as a new political party, Coldwell's approach proved inadequate. Douglas was defeated in the provincial election by the Liberal candidate.

Douglas learned his lesson, and he immediately began to

devise that style of campaign oratory which was to bring him victory after victory in Saskatchewan, and which would later endear him to Canadians across the country when he spoke as leader of the NDP (even if they didn't vote for him). Douglas did not "pander to the emotions", but he did seek to reduce sometimes dry economic and social doctrine into more easily understood terms. He borrowed from the Bible, naturally, and presented the CCF goals and platform in the form of parables and stories...and always with a touch of humour. Douglas found that humour was just as valuable as clothing and food in the Dirty Thirties. It raised the peoples' spirits and lightened their considerable burdens. At the same time, the Douglas sense of humour gave people confidence about the CCF...the party *could not* be such a threat to society if it was represented by a man with such a human sense of humour.

A typical Douglas parable during the federal election of 1935 and subsequent ones, was the tale of the cream separator. As Douglas told it, it went something like this (there were variations for every crowd and every occasion).

Sometimes, he would say, while he was out giving campaign speeches and meeting with rural people at remote farm communities throughout Saskatchewan, he'd find himself invited for dinner at a farm house. And, naturally, he'd pitch in to help with the dinner chores. Usually, the farm wife would give him the job of turning the cream separator because it was an easy job and one that he couldn't make a mistake doing. Tommy would confess that often he hummed "Onward Christian Soldiers" as he turned the handle of the cream separator in order to prevent boredom. But...the longer he looked at the cream separator, the more it reminded him of how society was running. The farmers poured in the good fresh milk. The city workers turned the crank of the machine, and the products came out of two spouts: heavy rich cream for a few who could afford it, and skimmed-off milk for everyone else. And, Tommy would conclude, when the guys at the top got a belly-ache from eating all that cream they'd hold up a hand and say 'Stop! Hold it! No more milk. This is a Depression.'

Another of Douglas's favourite parables was about Mouseland.

Every four years in Mouseland, it being a democratic country, the mice held an election. One year they would elect the
black cats. And conditions — for mice — were terrible. So
in four years they rose up in protest, threw out the black
cats, and — elected white cats. The white cats preyed on the
mice even more terribly than their predecessors had. So next
time — back in went the black ones.

   Until one day, a small mouse stood up in his corner and
proposed, "Let us elect *mice*." They called him a radical, a
Communist, a National Socialist. But the idea spread. Mice
got the message. The day came. . .[16]

It was with this sort of presentation, alternated with very
accurate and detailed social and economic appraisals, that won
Douglas a federal seat in the 1935 election.

It has become not only fashionable, but almost obligatory, to
regard the Douglas style of campaign oratory as "corny" —
simplistic and suited only to a politically naive electorate such as
the Saskatchewan electorate *must* have been. This viewpoint is
an eastern pretension and myth, which should be obvious on a
moment's objective reflection about the sort of simplistic politics
"sophisticated" easterners have swallowed from the mouths of
people like George Drew, Mike Pearson, Bill Davis and Pierre
Trudeau . . . not to mention Brian Mulroney. The fact is that
during the Thirties the Saskatchewan electorate proved capable
of distinguishing between various different parties, all calling
themselves "socialist", and choosing the CCF because they were
not confounded by labels. They distinguished between "National
Socialism" (Nazis), Social Credit, the democratic socialism
represented by the Co-operative Commonwealth Federation and
virulent anti-democratic Communism, and this, in spite of the
best Liberal efforts to discredit the CCF by equating them with
Nazis and Bolsheviks in campaign literature. One Liberal statement issued on January 27, 1944 said:

There has emerged out of the Coldwell fog the true charac-
ter of national socialism, its statism and its sameness with
the Communism of Tim Buck's Labour-Progressive
Party.[17]

It was a unique experience, even for the CCF which was used

to name-calling, to be labelled *both* Nazi and Communist in the same sentence. Saskatchewan voters of the Thirties and Forties learned to differentiate, while the voters of Ontario never did. Tactics of political libel worked very well in Ontario and succeeded in confusing the electorate about the type of party the CCF was.

The truth of the matter is that economic disaster, plus rural isolation, had bred in the Saskatchewan electorate a hungry appetite for political literature of all sorts. They even devoured *Hansard!* Cautionary tales are still current, among Liberals and PCs, about the "sophisticated" eastern politician stumping through rural Saskatchewan and trying to wool-pull local farmers about what he said and did in Parliament...and the begrimed farmer at some meeting pulling a well-thumbed copy of *Hansard* from his cover-alls and quoting back to the politician what he *actually* said in Parliament. No doubt, most of the stories are aprocryphal, but they were used to illustrate a truth — that the rural electorate of Saskatchewan had become self-educated in politics to a degree well beyond the supposed "sophistication" of other provincial constituencies.

Douglas's stories were not "corn" within this milieu or any other. His parables distilled the essence of a rather novel and very complicated political and social ideology. His humour was not only a mechanism to make the parables more understandable and digestible, but was intended to lighten the burdens and worries of the Depression. His listeners, the prairies farmers and workers, bore the full brunt of the worst hardships of the Dirty Thirties.

In the 1936 federal election, his second campaign and first successful one, Douglas learned that politics was a hard game when played by Liberal rules. Douglas was able to buy an automobile by establishing a raffle so that the car would be won by some Saskatchewan CCF voter at the end of the campaign. This car, a Whippet, enabled him to travel throughout his large rural riding. On several occasions, Liberal saboteurs tried to wreck this vital transportation by adding sand or sugar to the gas tank. Douglas learned the hard way that the filler-cap had to be locked. Then, at a later stage of the campaign, the rear wheel nuts were loosened on the Whippet in an effort to promote an accident on the highways. But the final act of the Liberal opponent was to break in to the printing shop where CCF pamphlets were being produced in an effort to find out advanced information about what Douglas would say next. It was a final act, because this strategem backfired in 1936. The RCMP was informed of the break-in and, perhaps surprisingly, began an investigation which led to the Liberal candidate and his supporters. The voters decided that they did not want to elect a thief to Parliament and Douglas won his seat in Ottawa. This Saskatchewan "Watergate" was the first big break for Tommy Douglas.

For Douglas and the CCF in Ottawa, the years between 1936 and 1944 were, of course, dominated by the gathering storm of war in Europe and the inevetible breaking of the deluge. This was traumatic time for the CCF, perhaps more than for other parties, because of its general anti-war stance and because of the very determined pacificism of the CCF leader, J.S. Woodsworth. Woodsworth remained steadfastly opposed to Canada's entry into the war. It was a position not only at odds with the emotional sentiments of the country as a whole, but one at odds with the position of Douglas and the other CCF members. While granting that the war exhibited many of the usual symptoms and motivations of capitalist economic exploitation, Douglas was also aware that Hitlerite Germany represented a phenomenon of another order, something beyond the pale of 20th Century social struggles, and could only be dealt with through the application of counter-force. Douglas himself tried to enlist with the Winnipeg Grenadiers, which incorporated some men from Saskatchewan, but was finally rejected because of the osteomyelitis problem with his leg.

The position of Douglas and the remainder of the CCF group in Ottawa was to attempt to ensure that there would be "no conscription of men without an equal conscription of wealth". The CCF did not want thousands of people to be sacrificed while industrialists made fortunes on war profiteering. In short, Douglas and the CCF didn't want the necessity for defeating Hitler to be used as an excuse for capitalist war economics.

Douglas proposed to Parliament that war materiels would be produced in Canada at a fixed profit of just 5 per cent. Mackenzie King agreed to approach Canadian industrialists on that basis. It seems at least possible that Mackenzie King himself was sympathetic to the social justice represented by the Douglas idea. But it was a failure. As King himself reported to Parliament through C.D. Howe: "I can say to my honourable friend that from that day to this the Defence Purchasing Board has done its very best to place contracts on that basis (i.e. 5 per cent profit), and has used every pressure that could be brought to bear in the form of patriotism and so on, but to date it has not succeeded in placing a single contract on that basis."[18]

"It was scandalous," Douglas said. "The arms manufacturers actually went on strike. If the workers, or the soldiers, had taken such a position, think of the outcry!"[19]

While there is some indication that the Prime Minister, Mackenzie King, was himself personally sympathetic to the CCF stance and the 5 per cent solution, there's ample indication that C.D. Howe and the Liberal Party as a whole viewed the war as just another, and much better, opportunity for making money and dispensing patronage. A contract to manufacture Bren guns was awarded to a very small company on a pure patronage basis, and this contract caused a scandal when it came to light . . . but, of course, there were many more such contracts that never came under public scrutiny. Then, after the war, it was C.D. Howe who made a personal deal with an American company for the construction of a trans-Canada pipeline, a deal whereby the construction would be 90 per cent paid for by Canadian taxpayers, while the ownership of the completed pipeline would remain in "private" (and American) hands. Personally sympathetic perhaps, but Mackenzie King was not about to curtail the time-honoured antics of his party.

The CCF had two other major concerns during the war years. The first and most pressing emotionally for the people of Canada was to ensure the welfare of the fighting people overseas. The second concern, just as pressing but lacking the emotional content, was to ensure that there would be no post-war economic slump as there had been in 1919, to ensure that the thousands of returning soldiers could obtain jobs or that, at least, social programs softened unemployment for soldiers' families. Douglas became the most active CCF spokesman and activist on both issues.

Some Canadians forces, including elements of the Winnipeg Grenadiers, were sent to Hong Kong to support the British garrison there and they arrived just in time to be defeated, killed and captured by invading Japanese forces. Douglas had cause to know, having trained briefly with the Winnipeg Grenadiers, that the men were ill-equipped and ill-trained. He demanded, and received, and inquiry. The resulting 5½-page report was, in Douglas's view a white-wash, and he threatened an exposé on the floor of the House . . . at which point Mackenzie King requested a private meeting. Knowing that something was in the wind, Douglas refused to meet with King without taking along a witness, Coldwell. King agreed to the terms. In the Prime Minister's office, Douglas and Coldwell were shown secret government files which, for King and the Liberals, adequately explained the tragedy. British Intelligence had guaranteed the Canadian government that Japan was not about to launch any imminent aggression in the Pacific in late 1941! And that's why the half-trained and badly-equipped men from the prairies had been sent to Hong Kong. The plan had been to complete their training and equipping while they were serving garrison duty in "peaceful" Hong Kong. The King government, because of colonial and emotional ties with Britain, had trusted British Intelligence assurances and knuckled under the British pressure to supply troops.

Douglas pointed out that American Intelligence had warned of imminent Japanese action around the Pacific as early as October 1941 . . . but Canada had preferred to rely on the Brits. Douglas suggested that Canada should start its own military intelligence agency rather than relying on the British and he exposed the entire fiasco in the Commons, refusing to let King and the Liberals become a "bomb-proof shelter" for the incompetence of British Intelligence or for the ruthless machinations of Churchill.

Again, later in 1942, Douglas wondered why the British naval and air bombardment had ended prematurely in the Dieppe raid and Canadian soldiers were sent in to be butchered.

> He pressed the question so hard that at one point Defence Minister Ralston rose with a folder in his hands and said that if he really wanted that information he could have it. King silenced him before he could continue. Douglas was convinced that effective command of Canadian troops had

been taken out of Canadian hands, and the much-prized independence of Canada's war effort was demolished by the British attitude toward its former colony.[20]

Douglas, all through the war years, questioned the Canadian colonial mentality that allowed Britain, on more than one occasion, to use Canadian troops (and those of other Commonwealth nations) as cannon fodder in a British war effort that was often inept and incompetent. Needless to say, Douglas's criticisms were labelled as being "disloyal" and "unpatriotic" by some political opponents.

But the major concern of Douglas and the CCF was the post-war world. The CCF did not want a repetition of the post-World War I unemployment and Depression, and there were enough Canadians who remembered the former era to be concerned as well, especially among the Canadian forces overseas. As various writers have noted, Canadians didn't march off to World War II with the blind and naive patriotism that characterized World War I. They marched off, but out of a sense of grim duty and with a wary and somewhat cynical eye on their government and military leaders. As the outcome of the war in Europe became a certainty of victory for the Allies, Canadians at home and in the services began to take the CCF's ideology more seriously than ever.

The Gallup Poll showed CCF support rising in a high curve: 10 per cent in January 1942; 21 per cent in September 1942; 23 per cent in February 1943, and a delirious 29 per cent in September 1943, at which point it topped the poll, a percentage point ahead of the Liberals and Conservatives.[21]

In short, by late in the war, the CCF was the most popular party (according to polls) in Canada. There seemed to be a real possibility of coming to power in both provincial governments and in Ottawa. In the Ontario provincial election of 1943, the CCF moved from no seats to 34... becoming the Official Opposition.

But it was in Saskatchewan, which had always been the centre of CCF power, that the party saw a realistic chance of forming the government. Douglas decided to return to provincial politics to try to win a CCF victory in Saskatchewan. Since the CCF had been the Official Opposition in that province since 1938, given the poll results, there was a strong chance of forming a CCF government.

The Liberal Premier of Saskatchewan had won the election of 1938, but the mood of the mid-forties scared him. He sought ways of postponing a confrontation with the CCF at the polls. . .

> In 1943 he had two Independent M.L.A.s introduce a bill, which the government accepted, prolonging the Legislature's life to six years, because of the exigencies of war![22]

Tommy Douglas later commented on this unconstitutional Liberal strategy for defeating the CCF:

> If he had called the election in '42 or '43 we would have had a close call, either way. By the end of '43 the tide had turned and nothing could save him.
> Mackenzie King told me privately he had written to Patterson warning him, saying he ought to go to the country: he was violating all the democratic principles we were supposed to be fighting for, and every day he was inviting more disaster.[23]

The election in Saskatchewan was finally called for 1944, and it proved a disaster for the Liberals. The CCF won 47 of 52 seats and formed the first social democratic government in Canada... "a beachhead of socialism on a continent of capitalism", as the rhetoric of the period would have it. In all of the elections of the mid-forties, the service vote was heavily CCF and instrumental not only in bringing the CCF to power in Saskatchewan, but also in accounting for some disquieting political upsets which caused the Liberal establishment in Ottawa to do some hard thinking.

> The votes of the men and women in the armed forces went heavily to the CCF, which took 60 per cent to the Liberal's 28. The same trend would show up in the federal election the following year. Mackenzie King lost his seat in Prince Albert in 1945, his advantage wiped out by the service vote. Prince Albert put up a sign on its outskirts, a souvenir of

European battles: "This town liberated by the Canadian Army".[24]

It was only by adroit adoption of CCF social and economic policy by Liberals and Conservatives that the "establishment" was able to stave off a very real threat of CCF government in several provinces and even in Ottawa.

But in Saskatchewan, which did go CCF in 1944, Douglas experienced the same old Liberal brand of campaigning he'd first confronted a decade before. The three major dailies in the province were all Liberal-owned and operated during the election in a way that made a mockery of calling the Canadian press "responsible". Since the Gallup polls showed a substantial CCF lead in Saskatchewan and predicted a CCF victory, the dailies simply refused to print the Gallup results. Instead, their own polls, described as "the consensus of opinion of a number of electors", showed the Liberals ahead and certain to form the next government. The CCF organizers had to bring in out-of-province newspapers to communicate the actual state of affairs to the electors of Saskatchewan.

The Regina *Leader-Post* wanted the CCF to openly "admit" that the party would use democracy to obtain power, but would then institute a dictatorship.

> Why does not Mr. (David) Lewis come out frankly and say that the CCF socialists will use democracy to obtain power, but will scrap it as soon as they get into office."[25]

But, as Shackleton observed in her biography of Douglas, this Liberal strategem, too, backfired.

> Since the Liberal Administration was the only one in the country to illegally prolong its own life without going to the country, such editorials were fuel to CCF public speeches. Douglas gave a solemn promise to hold an election every four years in the month of June, a promise he carefully observed.[26]

But his blatant contradiction of fact about Liberal respect for democracy did not prevent the *Leader-Post* from printing dire warnings on the eve of the election. According to this rag, the election of the CCF "would vitally affect the way of living of every individual, will affect the right to own and use property" and, further, the CCF would institute a "stultifying and dictatorial system" that would "start Canada on the road to strife and devastation that has been followed by European countries."[27]

A CCF worker, T.H. McLeod, describes the affect of the massive CCF victory on those Liberals who had succumbed to the dangerous practice of believing their own propaganda.

> It was a terrible shock to the Liberals. There were people on the street, Liberals I knew quite well, *crying*. Many believed their own propaganda, the tales that if the CCF was elected they would take over your insurance, all you'd paid in would be confiscated. If you were a farmer the CCF would take over your land — all the work you'd put in improving your property would be lost. Very few people in their right minds believed that — but there were very few Liberals in their right mind at that time! Those grown men standing there crying! What the hell had produced this state of mind in those people?[28]

Douglas watched the election results being chalked up with a realistic appreciation of the problems that the CCF victory would bring:

> I watched the results in the committee room in the Weyburn Legion Hall. I was fully conscious of what we were starting in to. A province with the second highest per capita debt, the second lowest per capita income! Patterson had said we were a bankrupt province; we hadn't been able to borrow a dollar on the open market since 1932.
>
> In had no illusions that I was starting on a honeymoon.
>
> But I wasn't alarmed. When you're young you think you can lick anything.
>
> I kept remembering what the farmers had said. If you can just save our farms; if you can just do that much.[29]

Saving the farms from mortgage companies was the CCF's first priority, and the Farm Security Act of 1944 was one of the first bills passed. "It protected the home quarter against foreclosure, and suspended mortgage payments during years of crop failure, defined as those years when, for reasons beyond the farmer's control, he received a cash return of less than six dollars per acre sown to grain."[30] But the Act of 1944 also went a bit further... it suspended interest payments on mortgages during years of crop failure.

While possibly willing to consider suspension of mortgage payments during years of crop failure, the eastern establishment was not willing to consider the suspension of interest on the mortgages. Financial lobbyists in Ottawa pressured the federal government to disallow the CCF's Farm Security Act, claiming that it infringed upon "sacredness of contract". Another CCF bill added to the Ottawa furor — legislation to tax unused mineral rights on the *ten million acres* of Saskatchewan land which the Canadian Pacific Railway had been granted to "tempt" the building of the trans-Canada railroad.

> The federal government's right to disallow provincial legislation has been used at irregular intervals. The cases where it has been employed are noteworthy for two reasons. Disallowance has always been used against a provincial government of a different political stripe. Secondly, the legislation in question has generally had to do with business and financial interests. Human rights infringements, even breaches of the constitution (as when the Liberal government of Saskatchewan extended its own life by an unlawful twelve months) went unremarked and unchallenged. Aberhart's attempt to manipulate credit in Alberta was swiftly quashed; Duplessis' infamous Padlock Law in Quebec was ignored, and left to the action of private citizens and the courts.
> In September 1945 the Douglas government was informed that it had three weeks to prepare a defence of its legislation before the Ottawa hearings.[31]

Douglas and the CCF began to prepare their legal defence of the legislation, but also began to prepare the defence for their moral stance for the people of Saskatchewan. Since Douglas and the CCF were denied access to the Saskatchewan network of the Canadian Broadcasting Corporation, the message was communicated over commercial radio stations.

Douglas told the radio audience:

We have just finished a war which was fought, we were told,

for the preservation of democratic insitutions. It would appear that the war is not finished. We have simply moved the battlefields from the banks of the Rhine to the prairies of Saskatchewan.

If corporations can have these laws disallowed then there are no laws passed by a free legislature which they cannot have set aside. Where then is our boasted freedom? Why elect governments if Bay Street and St. James Street are to have the power to decide what laws shall stand and what laws shall fail? We have reached a time of supreme testing in this province.

Let me issue a word of warning to those who are moving heaven and earth to have this legislation disallowed. I want to tell them that they are not dealing in this case with a government of tired old men who are merely holding onto power for the spoils of office with a hope of finding a final resting place in the Senate. They are dealing with a government fresh from the people with a mandate to carry out the people's wishes. Those wishes will be carried out. If these vested interests succeed in persuading the Federal Government to disallow this legislation we still have other resources at our disposal and we will not hesitate to use them. . .

We are prepared to lead the fight if you are prepared to follow us into battle.[32]

And the people of Saskatchewan followed the CCF into this, the first of several major battles. Protests poured into Ottawa by letter and telegram, mass meetings were organized throughout the province. The federal government made a decision to forget about trying disallowance. But the private interests didn't give up and took their case to the courts, and even to the final arbiter, the Privy Council of Great Britain. Their argument was that the exemption of interest payments during years of crop failure was beyond the powers of a provincial government under the provisions of the British North America Act. This view was eventually upheld in the Supreme Court, with one dissenting opinion, but the major provisions of the Farm Security Act went unchallenged.

Another of the CCF's priorities, and another cause for confrontation (but with a surprising adversary) concerned rural electrification. Douglas was determined to bring the convenience and labour-saving of electricity to Saskatchewan farms as quickly as possible, largely because he'd been personally moved by the brutality hard work that fell upon the farm wives. It is hard for most Canadians to realize that much of Saskatchewan did not have electricity until the 1950s. The CCF eventually brought electricity to 47,000 farm families in the province.

The vehicle for this was the nationalized Power Corporation which was established in line with the provisions of the Regina Manifesto to nationalize utilities.

One of Douglas's major confrontations had to do with the unionized workers of his own Power Corporation, and it was a confrontation that deeply troubled the entire CCF — but for different reasons. The "religious" component of the CCF, personified by Douglas and some other western political leaders actually in power in Saskatchewan, were troubled at the thought of one segment of society, in this case the union, wanting an unfair share of the available economic pie. Douglas made it clear to the union that Saskatchewan could not raise Power Corporation wages beyond an already-fair level *and* continue to bring electricity to more rural farms.

The eastern "Marxist" components of the CCF, personified by David Lewis, and other organizers and intellectuals who were not actually in power in any elected capacity, were appalled at the thought that a socialist government would even consider taking a hard line on workers . . . especially its own workers.

But Douglas took a hard line indeed. He threatened compulsory arbitration and, if that didn't work, legislation ordering the union not to strike. At the eleventh hour, Douglas shrewdly found a way to avert a CCF rift and bring the union to an agreement that would not compromise the rural electrification program. He gave *David Lewis* the job of negotiating a settlement. It was an offer that Lewis "couldn't refuse" even though he might have wanted to. As Lewis described it, the "Douglas solution" took him by surprise:

I was in Windsor. I got a call from Tommy who informed me Neil Reimer (Canadian Director of the Oil Worker's International Union) was on an extension, and they both wanted me to go out to mediate the dispute. I asked 'Why me?' and there were two laughs on the line. It was probably Tommy's idea. He told me, 'You're the national president of the CCF so you can't possibly do the CCF in, and as a labour lawyer acting for the same union in Ontario you can't possibly do the union in, so we think you're the right guy' . . .

It was typical of Tommy's acute judgement. Most people would have have said I was impossible for the job because of my double role. But I did settle it. I met with them for eight or nine days, and there was no strike. Exactly what Tommy predicted did happen. I was able to get away with saying to labour, 'Stop being bloody fools' and I was able to tell management, 'you'd better go back and tell the government this isn't acceptable'. It worked out.[33]

Yes, it worked out . . . but it also demonstrated another level of the "Marxist vs. Methodist" contradiction inherent in the old CCF and, to some degree, in the younger NDP. It was the contradiction between "labour" and "farmers", the uneasy coalition of both that seemed the only solution in the Dirty Thirties, but which seemed to be less of a bond as time passed. In Saskatchewan just before the union's dispute with Tommy Douglas, labour's "regard" for the rural population of Saskatchewan is best illustrated by an excerpt of a Douglas letter to Neil Reimer. Douglas complained about another representative of the Oil Workers' International Union, Alex McAuslane:

Mr. McAuslane advised the two ministers of the Government whom he met last fall that the farm electrification program should be scrapped since it was this expensive program which had reduced their (Power Corporation's) surplus to a nominal amount and was preventing an across-the-board wage increase. These two ministers also informed me that Mr. McAuslane advised them that if they could not make bigger surpluses than they were now getting they should turn the power operations of the province over to private enterprise who could probably show a much better profit.[34]

So much for the social conscience of organized labour! The wages of the OWIU, which were already equal to industry standards, should be raised even at the cost of rural electrification.

Back in the early 1930s Douglas had worked on behalf of the unions in Estevan because they were being unfairly treated. In the late 1940s and early 1950s he had to curb the unions attempts to treat other segments of society unfairly. Douglas's motivation, throughout his political career, was the welfare of people within a Christian perspective. It was David Lewis, operating from a Marxist ideological and doctrinaire perspective, who seemed quite willing to sacrifice rural electrification in Saskatchewan for the greater glory of building a CCF-Labour coalition at all costs. It was Lewis who was disturbed that Douglas might actually pass anti-strike legislation. It was unthinkable, from a doctrinaire viewpoint... necessary from a Christian compassionate viewpoint. As Douglas succinctly put it when outlining his determination to legislate against a strike if necessary:

> It is 25 degrees below zero this morning in Saskatchewan. Thousands of homes are entirely dependent on power and gas to operate their heating facilities... Much as we would dislike making arbitration compulsory, I think you will agree that it would be an act of complete irresponsibility for us to stand idly by and permit a strike.[35]

The philosophical schism between "Marxism" and "Methodism", between religious motivation and ideological-doctrine motivation, and between labour and farm, is at the core of the NDP's failure as a national party. Not that a large percentage of the Canadian population is rural any longer, but the quality of human compassion somehow generated and developed on the prairies between 1930-1960 is still very much a commodity to be appreciated, a rather more valuable commodity than Marxist dialectics when it comes to winning the hearts and spirits of Canadian voters. It may very well be that the NDP cannot become a major Canadian political party until and unless it manages to revive some of the Douglas-style religious commitment and compassion and jettisons much of the Marxist mechanistic, non-human outlook on history and what makes it.

Another confrontation faced by the CCF in Saskatchewan concerned the imposition of Medicare and the organized opposition mounted by the province's doctors. Medicare was, perhaps, the social program closest to Tommy Douglas's own heart. He himself became the Minister of Health in his own government, determined to see Medicare established in the Saskatchewan social commonwealth. His program was not based on ignorant, if well-intentioned, social commitment. The first step was a survey of the needs and the type of program that would best fill them within the province's resources. Douglas appointed Dr. Henry E. Sigerist to undertake the preliminary survey.

> "Dr. Sigerist was teaching at Sir Johns Hopkins," Douglas said. "He was probably the greatest authority in the world on social medicine. He had a great personality, he got along well with everyone, and he was intrigued by the situation in Saskatchewan and its long record in public health programs — the first anti-tuberculosis program in Canada, started by Saskatchewan farm women — so he came for two years and actually stayed for five. And we got other outstanding people, Dr. Len Rosenfeldt, Dr. Cecil and Dr. Mendel Sheps — Cecil was in the army but we got him out. And the great prize was Dr. Fred Mott!
> When Sigerist made his first report I said, 'Great. Now where can we get the people to put it into effect? Who is the best man in North America?' Sigerist said, 'Fred Mott. But you can't get him. I said, 'Why not? He said, 'He happens to be the Assistant Surgeon-General of the United States Army'".[36]

Douglas got Dr. Fred Mott, naturally. Mott quickly assembled a team to draft the parameters of a comprehensive hospital insurance program to become effective on January 1, 1947. It was a crash program. Mott once protested that it could not be done within the Douglas schedule, but Douglas insisted that it had to be done . . . and it was.

> The Hospital Insurance Plan began as promised on New Year's Day 1947, with Douglas and Dr. Fred Mott on hand at Regina General Hospital to see the first patient admitted under the scheme at a little after midnight.[37]

Douglas, the compassionate social reformer and successful politician allowed the politician's sensibilities to come out when he later admitted his relief that the first patient under the scheme was an expectant mother . . . it was "fortunately a joyful occasion, she was having a child."

The cost of Saskatchewan's hospital insurance program was set at $5 per person and $10 per family per year. Initially, Douglas and the CCF were deluged with letters from voters complaining at the cost because they, personally, had never spent "a day in the hospital" and didn't see why they should pay for others who did. But, by 1948, Douglas's CCF government was returned for its second term in office largely on the very visible benefits of the hospital insurance scheme.

The next step in Medicare was not just hospital insurance, but a comprehensive system of insurance for all *necessary* health needs. Typically, Douglas had started with the most acute problem, the guarantee of adequate paid hospitalization ... but he intended to proceed with the socialization of all health services short of the need for hospitalization. And, in accordance with his philosophy of gradualism in institutionalizing social change, he almost waited too long. It was not until 1959 that Douglas announced the introduction of Medicare. It was based on five principles: prepayment, universal coverage; high quality of service; administration by a public body responsible to the legislature; and "in a form acceptable both to those providing the service and those receiving it".

It is instructive to note that the Liberal opposition in the Saskatchewan legislature had been twitting Douglas about the CCF's government's delay in introducing Medicare. Douglas responded:

> We don't need the Opposition to remind us. I made a pledge with myself long before I ever sat in this house, in the years when I knew something about what it means to get health services when you didn't have the money to pay for them. I made a pledge that if I ever had anything to do with it, people would be able to get health services just as they are able to get educational services, as an inalienable right of being a citizen of a Christian country.[38]

And, naturally, once Douglas did introduce Medicare, the Saskatchewan doctors revolted and the Liberal Official Opposition supported them after criticizing the CCF's delay in establishing the program.

The practical political problem was simply that too much time had elapsed between the first articulation of the Medicare idea and its implementation. Many doctors would have supported Medicare in the dark days of the 1930s and 1940s because it would have guaranteed them some payment for the services they were bound to offer under their Hippocratic Oath. The hospitalization insurance scheme of 1947 offered them a guarantee of payment as well. But, by 1959, times had changed because of 15 years of war-induced prosperity. Doctors did not want their fee schedules regulated by government. There was, at that time, not much problem in getting paid. Coldwell stated the case plainly: "The doctors are more concerned here with maintaining high fees than serving the people of Saskatchewan."

The doctors fought Medicare, and not just individually. The College of Physicians and Surgeons of Saskatchewan organized a "compulsory opposition" to the CCF scheme, assessing all the doctors in Saskatchewan $100 to pay the costs of College-printed literature to oppose the program. It was "not a voluntary assessment", as the College made clear. The doctors used scare tactics, based on "suggestions" emanating from the College. For example, in dealing with nervous women, the College literature proposed the following doctor-to-patient speech:

> Many times we have sat down in our office with a woman and discussed emotional situations which crop up during pregnancy or other critical periods in a woman's life. We know that under Government administration we would be prevented from rendering these vital services ... It could very easily be that this type of condition (tension during menopause) must be referred to a psychiatric clinic or a mental hospital, a situation which we, as your personal physician, would deplore.[39]

In addition to suggesting the middle-aged women that menopausal tension "might" be justification for "referring" them to a mental hospital under Medicare, the good doctors of Saskatchewan were fond of telling pregnant women that "this might be the last pre-natal check-up they could have" before Medicare was enforced.

And, in the end, the doctors of Saskatchewan went on strike.

The Douglas response to the doctors was the same as his response to the OWIU over the Power Corporation wage dispute... he confronted them. British doctors were airlifted into Saskatchewan to provide "interim" medical care, and it was made not altogether unclear that this "interim" care could be extended indefinitely since a number of British physicians were not averse to a new career in Canada. At the same time, Douglas advised the doctors to get back to their real job of healing, instead of scaring vulnerable patients. Medicare was finally established in Saskatchewan, and all across Canada, although there have been continuing and persistent attempts by some doctors and politicians to undermine the universal nature of it.

In his last Saskatchewan provincial election, in 1960, Douglas again won for the CCF and concluded 16 years of social democratic government in Saskatchewan. By that time, even the establishment papers had learned to respect him. After the 1960 election in Saskatchewan, Jack Scott of the Vancouver *Sun* wrote:

> This man Douglas — well, how'll I put it? He's a good deed in a naughty world. He's a breath of clean prairie air in a stifling climate of payola and chicanery and double-talk and pretence, global and local.
>
> Forget the politics. Here's a man who wanted to do something for the human race. He chose the method that seemed best to him, quarrel with it if you will. He was motivated by an ideal.
>
> To call him a politician, as you'd call Bennett or Diefenbaker a politician, is to insult him. He was and is a dreamer and a humanitarian, incorruptible, genuine and intellectually honest.[40]

And so Tommy Douglas remains today. His battles, triumphs and defeats, were not over with his last Saskatchewan election of 1960. More battles awaited him, but not as leader of the Saskatchewan CCF. His later battles were fought as leader of the New Democratic Party.

But before going into the more recent history of the NDP between 1961 and 1985, it may be helpful to wonder about the qualities of T.C. Douglas that made him more than a politician and to wonder about the source of his commitment to the service of humanity. We cannot escape taking a look at the Order of Jacques De Molay.

* * * * * *

At this point it might be enough to just say that Tommy Douglas possessed those qualities of compassion that led him to make a lifelong commitment for social justice, and that this "humanist" philosophy greatly molded the founding ideals of the CCF which have, in turn, had a profound affect on the political structure of Canadian politics.

But it might also be appropriate to examine the origins of his "humanist" philosophy. If indeed, Tommy Douglas's convictions have had this influence on Canadian political thought, then it may not be just an interesting diversion to trace historically the teachings of the Masons and De Molay Society which so greatly influenced him as a young man.

The historical evolution of the present day Masons and De Molay Society can be traced all the way back to the end of the 11th Century when Christian crusaders had wrested much of the Holy Land from the Islamic Saracens and, when in the year 1099 A.D., a rather obscure French nobleman by the name of Godfroi de Bouillon was named King of Jerusalem by "an anonymous conclave"[41] of clerics and secular leaders. The ascension of de Bouil lon's line to the throne of Jerusalem has somewhat puzzled later historians. It apparently bothered no one at the time, and it seems that the Bouillon, at least, knew what was going to happen before he left Europe on the Crusade. He gave up his lands and titles in Europe. He allied himself and the fortunes of his House to Palestine. The newly-created Kingdom of Jerusalem was accounted equal to the most illustrious European royalty.

Nineteen years later, the second King of Jerusalem, Baudoin (Godfroi's younger brother), established the famous Order of the Temple, better known as the "Knights Templar".

The Knights Templar have loomed more mysteriously in history than even the curious elevation of Godfroi de Bouillon to the throne of Jerusalem.

At first, there were only nine knights of the Temple and for nine years no other recruits were admitted. The mandate of these knights was to protect pilgrims on all the roads of the Holy Land. Aside from the fact that their numbers were wholly inadequate to perform such a task, there is no record of the Knights Templar actually protecting any pilgrims in Palestine.[42]

Yet within a very short time the new order had gained enormous prestige in Europe. Saint Bernard spoke highly of the Templars and a papal decree made them answerable only to the Pope and independent of all secular authority.

Although individual knights of the Order were sworn to poverty and to a strict code of behaviour drafted by Saint Bernard himself, the Knights Templar immediately began to amass great wealth. They very quickly accumulated financial resources that enabled them to become the bankers of their age. They built protected warehouses all over Europe in which merchants could store their goods in safety. They loaned money and they revived the ancient practice of issuing and honouring letters of credit, cheques, so that merchants could avoid carrying large amounts of bulky and tempting money around with them. Whether or not the Templars did much for pilgrim traffic in the Holy Land, it is certain thay they encouraged the growth of trade and commerce in Europe.

Because the Templars were independent of all secular authority, they could pursue their banking and warehousing throughout Europe, irrespective of the wishes of the local noble who thought he controlled things. The Templars betrayed the very class they supposedly represented, at least in an economic and political sense.

In addition to being unorthodox in an economic and political sense in Europe, they were also apparently unorthodox in matters of religion. It was not long before their initial aura of sanctity was transformed, among the already financially disgruntled nobility, into suspicions of heresy.

In the year 1187 A.D., after less than a century of Christian rule, Jerusalem and much of the Holy Land was recovered by the Moslems. The dynasty established by Godfroi de Bouillon lost much of its prestige along with its throne. And along with the loss of its "geopolitical power base", Godfroi's line lost its security. The Templars, whose fortunes and *raison d'entre* were closely tied to the fortunes and curious power of the de Bouillon line, began to be regarded with less tolerance by both secular leaders and the Papacy.

Part of the reason for their loss of influence was the fact that the de Bouillon family was never trusted by the Roman Catholic church who only needed them as long as they could provide protection in the Holy Lands. This mistrust stemed from the fact that the de Bouillon clan was from a bloodline which arose in the South of France.

In the Pyrenees. During the 10th to 12th Centuries this area in the south of present-day France was the centre of a unique culture. It was unique in several ways. First of all, compared to most of Europe at the time, the civilization of Languedoc and Provence was advanced in the arts and sciences. There was much contact with the neighboring Moors across the Pyrenees, and much contact with the Jewish savants who lived among these Moors. Noble French families in the south inter-married across the Pyrenees.

The civilization in the south of France was advanced in terms of trade and economics, again because of close contact with the Moors who controlled much of the Mediterranean and all of the trade routes to the Far East. Languedoc and Provence were wealthy in relation to the rest of feudal Europe.

But the most profound way in which this southern French civilization differed from the rest of Europe was religious. It does not seem as if this civilization was really "Christian" at all in the way that term was understood then and is understood now. Or, if the civilization was Christian, its religion was a heresy.

The religion was called "Catharism" or the "Albigensian heresy" after the town of Albi which was a particular centre of this aberrant religion.

It is difficult to tell what Catharism really was, because all the accounts of it come from enemies of the religion. The Cathars themselves, and their own writings, were systematically destroyed by the victorious Roman Church.

At the "grassroots" or "village level" of participation, Catharism seems to have been vaguely Christian, or at least molded on the Christian model. There were Cathar churches operating in competition with Catholic ones. By about 1200 A.D., most of the population of Languedoc and Provence patronized Cathar churches in preference to Catholic ones. There were Roman churches in southern France where a Mass had not been said in several generations.

On the simplest level, the popularity of Catharism is easy to explain. The Roman clergy was corrupt and suffered by comparison with the Cathar "parfaits" or "perfected ones" who passed for Cathar clergy. Indeed, Saint Bernard, who travelled to Languedoc to preach against these heretics in 1145 A.D., was impressed by them: no sermons are more Christian than theirs, and their morals are pure", he wrote.

By "Christian", the good saint must have meant Christian *in spirit,* because the Albigensians certainly were not Christian *in dogma* according to the tenets of the Roman Church. Indeed, there are some who suspect that Saint Bernard was extremely impressed with the Cathars and became one, in secret . . .

Cathar "Christianity" rejected the death and Crucifixion of Jesus. Catharism rejected the idea of sacrifice, and perhaps even the idea of salvation, as these concepts are understood by modern Christians. Instead, the Cathars believed in the idea of living love, and the living love of Christ, and they therefore rejected the cross as a symbol of worship. Their symbol was the dove. Catharism also repudiated the idea of priests as intermediaries between God and man. The Albigensians had no priests.

Instead, the Cathars had religious, or "spiritual" leaders. These were called "parfaits" or, in Latin, *perfecti* . . . which means "perfects" or "perfected ones". These people were vowed to honesty, poverty, chastity and, apparently, vegetarianism. And they practised it. Where the Catholic priests were corrupt, the Cathar *perfecti* were not. Thus, by example, Catharism attracted the majority of the population of southern France who were drawn to their honesty and committment to the common man, qualities that the corrupt Catholic Papacy seemed to have forgotten. This "humanism" and compassion for fellow beings was not lost on the uneducated peasantry, and they had the respect and following of the majority of the population — a lesson some modern political leaders have used with great success. In any case, this growing popularity of the Cathars was not appreciated by the Papacy, and one of their ways of striking back was to absolve the "official status" they had given to the de Bouillon family and the Knights of Templar.

As well, the prosperous civilization of southern France excited the greed of the northern French barons. So long as Godfroi de Bouillon's line held a kingdom in the Holy Land, the prestige (plus the swords of the Templars) protected Godfroi's descendants and his "constituency" in the Pyrenees. But when Jerusalem was lost, hostile forces rapidly converged on Languedoc and Provence. Wealth was the motivator, but Cathar and Templar heresies were the pretexts.

In 1209 A.D., northern armies invaded the south in response to the Pope's call for a Crusade against the heretics. This was only 22 years after Godfroi's clan lost Jerusalem.

A protracted war of unparalleled ferocity raged for a third of a century until the last Cathar stronghold, Montsegur, fell in March of 1244. The Cathars were crushed. The heretics, the *parfaits,* died at flaming stakes or on the torture-racks of the victors. The Roman Church invented the Inquisition at this time, and interrogated the Cathars by particularly hideous means.

For a time, their sheer power — military, political and economic — prevented any overt moves against the Templars, even though many had participated in the defense of southern France, and even though many had died at Montsegur. But on Friday, October 13, 1307, King Philippe of France ordered simultaneous raids on Templar castles, priories and warehouses in his domain. Again, Templar wealth and a desire to break their power was the motivation, their unorthodoxies the excuse. By 1312, King Philippe had pressured Pope Clement V into disbanding the Templars. In 1314, *the last Grand Master of the Knights Templar, Jacques de Molay,* was roasted to death over a slow fire by order of King and Pope.

Templar wealth eluded the king. In addition to their own reputed treasure, it was widely believed that the Cathar treasure, or secret (believed to be the Holy Grail), had been passed on to the Templars after the fall of Montsegur. If so, the last Grand Master refused to reveal its location during his long agony.

The Templar fleet put out to sea from its port of La Rochelle a few hours before King Philippe's dawn raids of 1307. It has never been heard from since. It is a reasonable conjecture that this fleet carried the Templar treasures to safety, and perhaps the treasure of the Cathars as well.

The Templars who survived King Philippe's sudden strike against the Order dispersed to various countries outside of France. They were welcomed in many places. It is known that some fled to Scotland where they found refuge at Roslyn.[43]

The wealth and influence of the Templars ceased to exist, but not their beliefs in humanitarian service which have been passed on in time through an assortment of related orders, among them the Masons and Jacques De Molay Society.

Jacques de Molay was the last Grand Master of the Knights Templar. It is natural that the Order of De Molay would be a Masonic organization since many authorities consider the Freemasons to be one offshoot of the old Knights Templar.

The 20th Century Order of De Molay was established by a man named Frank Land in 1919. Land was a prominent Kansas City Mason and he hired a young teenager to work at odd jobs in the Masonic Lodge. The boy needed to work because his father had just died and the family needed whatever income the youngster could bring in. But one day this young man described the trouble that some of his friends were getting into, with little constructive to do, much unemployment and poverty. Land suggested that he invite his friends to the Masonic Lodge and they'd try to devise activities and discussions that might help deal with their problems. The boys did visit the Masonic Lodge and, one day, noted a portrait of Jacques de Molay in the Masonic Temple. They asked who he was, and why the Masons had a portrait of him. They were so inspired by his story that they decided to call their informal group after Jacques de Molay. Land thought about this, evidently considered it a good idea, and officially established the Order of De Molay as a junior Masonic organization in 1919.

It became a club to keep potentially "bad boys" out of trouble by giving them enjoyable and useful activities to perform. Like the Boy Scouts, the emphasis in the Order of De Molay was on public and social service.

The popularity of the Order was immediate and widespread. Chapters were quickly formed all across the United States and Canada. Winnipeg, where T.C. Douglas joined the Order, was one of the first Canadian cities to form a chapter.

Strangely enough, because of the personal antipathy of the Ontario Grand Master, the Order was banned within Ontario Masonry in 1935. The ban was lifted only in 1975 and, since then, several Ontario cities have begun to form chapters: London, Windsor, Ottawa and Toronto. But all across the U.S. and the rest of Canada, the Order became very popular in the era between the wars. Thousands of boys joined the Order, just as with Scouting, and some were active in both organizations. Tommy Douglas joined the Order and then also became a Scout Master. Aside from Tommy Douglas, other notable graduates of the Order include: Walt Disney, Walter Cronkite and Harry S. Truman. In fact, it seems that Disney's *Fantasia* incorporates a great deal of De Molay symbolism.

However, it must be understood that the Order of De Molay was not only and exactly analogous to the Boy Scouts. At higher levels of initiation, at least, it was something quite different. The fact of the matter is that the life of the Order's patron, Jacques de Molay, was totally committed to a great mission, which, when understood, compels a very different view of Western history and the basic forces which have dictated mankind's progress.

We do not know for sure how far Tommy Douglas was initiated into the secret history personified by Jacques de Molay when he was a member of the Winnipeg chapter. Tommy's biographer, Doris French Shackleton, tells us that Douglas became "Chaplain" of the Winnipeg chapter of the Order . . . but a Mason knowledgeable of the Order's history in Canada has informed me that Douglas was actually Master Counsellor of the Winnipeg chapter, the highest rank. Then, the incident that Shackleton relates, when Tommy played the part of Jacques de Molay in a "play", is actually a part of high initiation . . . a "rite", not just a "play" based on incidents in de Molay's life. In short, in the ceremony that Shackleton describes, the initiate *becomes* Jacques de Molay and commits his life to service in the same continuing crusade. That, possibly, is why Tommy Douglas's father was so moved that night according to Tommy's own recollections.

Whatever Douglas learned in the Order, and whatever he pledged on the night that he and and his father walked four miles in silence and the elder Tom acknowledged to Tommy that he "did no bad", it is undeniable that Douglas made his commitment to serving humanity as a minister and politician during the period that he was a member of the Order of Jacques De Molay.

It is therefore necessary to learn something of what inspired

Jacques de Molay and Tommy Douglas alike. What was the secret, and crusade, that both dedicated their lives to?

Again, at this point, it might be an interesting diversion to study the origins of Masonic beliefs, a "digression" that may turn out to be very relevant indeed. Once some idea of the secret history has been grasped, it should become apparent that the NDP has some chance for a resurgence in 1988, *but only if the party can find a philosophy and a leader that is attuned to the Tommy Douglas perspective on life and social change.*

We left the Knights of Templar fleeing for their lives from south France. It is known that the Templars fled to Scotland, after the dissolution of 1312, and it is known that some found refuge among the Saint-Clairs of Rosslyn in Midlothian. There is a Templar cemetery there. In the year 1345 a son was born to this lord of Rosslyn. The boy's name was Henry.

He became "a navigator", although his story is almost unknown. He voyaged upon the Atlantic. He discovered lands across the ocean. And it is recorded that he founded a city across the ocean, and stayed there until the founding was done, at the peril of his own House. He returned to Scotland just in time to die in the defence of his family. History has covered him.

There is no longer much doubt that the land he discovered was Nova Scotia. Even the Nova Scotia Museum accepts this.

The activities of Henry Sinclair are well recounted in Frederick Pohl's book, *Prince Henry Sinclair.* Pohl, almost single-handedly, has popularized an episode of history formerly known only to a few specialists. And it is an important episode because it involves nothing less that the European discovery of America more than a century before Columbus *and the establishment of a European colony on the American continent at the same time.*

Henry was born in 1345, about a generation after the Templar dispersal, into a family that had always been special paladins of de Bouillon's dynasty. Henry's ancestor and namesake, Henri de Saint-Clair, fought beside Godfroi de Bouillon at the taking of Jerusalem. Several Saint-Clairs became Templars themselves. The Sinclair lands were a Templar centre. What was more natural that that Rosslyn of the Sinclairs would become a Templar refuge? And what more natural than that the noble and powerful

Sinclairs would have become leaders of "neo-Templar" secret societies like the Freemasons and the Rosircrucians?

Henry Sinclair was born heir not only to Rosslyn, but also to the Earldom of Orkney. This earldom included the Shetland Islands as well as the Orkneys.

In becoming Earl of Orkney, Henry Sinclair became the first Sinclair to become a sea-chieftain. His island earldom demanded a navy in order to control it, and demanded an emphasis on shipping if its wealth was to be exploited. The most valuable resource of his new earldom was a fishing industry that brought in much more income than Rosslyn.

The Norwegian king "gave" Henry Sinclair the earldom to be held in fief, but it was, at first, something of a backhanded compliment. Although the Orkney and Shetland islands were owned and claimed by Norway, they had been independent in practice for some years. As the new Earl of Orkney, Henry's job was to regain control of the independent islanders. This entailed a mixture of warfare and diplomacy over almost 20 years. Henry proved exceedingly adept at both. By the time he could call himself Earl of Orkney in fact as well as in title, he really had become a sea-chieftain with an effective navy and with a good knowledge of maritime matters. And he'd become as much "Norse" as Norman French.

And this cultural transformation was most important. From his Viking-descended island subjects Sinclair not only obtained a corps of experienced sailors, but he also adopted their sturdy little ships that had evolved to cope with North Atlantic conditions. These ships themselves were descendants of Viking long ships.

Which brings us to the matter of the Viking voyages. Earl Henry was a prominent noble of Norway after his investiture as lord of the Isles. It is known that he made several journeys to Norway to be present at important state occasions. And, being a sea-lord and in close contact with the royal court in Norway, he could not have failed to hear of the Norse sagas of transatlantic exploration.

Not only that, but trade was still maintained between Norway and the old Viking colony in Greenland. Henry Sinclair must have learned much about the lands across the North Atlantic which had been seen and explored by Lief Ericsson, Thorfinn

Karlsefni, Thorall and other Northmen about 350 years earlier.

In short, in addition to sailors and ships, his Norse subjects and noble associates provided him with confirmation that there was land across the Atlantic to the west. His motives for initiating trans-atlantic voyages were not only rooted in the tradition of this "Norse" environment, but he also had another motive . . . to find and establish a refuge for the Templars away from the persecution of Europe.

Whether or not Henry Sinclair "discovered" America before Colombus is still a matter of some historical debate, but some authorities are convinced that this is exactly the case. His voyage is now accepted as fact by authorities such as Frederick Pohl, and if you visit the Nova Scotia Museum in Halifax, you can see the mural depicting Sinclair's voyage in which he discovered Nova Scotia in 1398.

There is also some evidence to suggest that Henry Sinclair named his new discovery "Arcadia" after his homeland the Earldom of Orkney, which at that time was known as "Orchadie".

I have covered the story of the Templars, Jacques de Molay, the Templar refugees of Rosslyn, Henry Sinclair and his voyage of 1398 to show that this secret history is supported by a substantial body of fact and connecting coincidences that can be studied by conventional historians. In spite of the fact that efforts have apparently been made to disguise and obscure this secret history, hints and clues remain.

If Henry Sinclair did, in fact, establish a religious refuge a century before the American continent was supposedly discovered by Columbus and Cabot, it would explain a number of puzzling and irritating minor mysteries about the early colonization of Canada and subsequent political and social development of North America. It is now the time to abbreviate the remaining outline of this secret history considerably, but it is necessary to sketch the entire story so that the significance of the De Bouillon clan and its supporters becomes apparent. By covering the period from 1099 A.D. and the taking of Jerusalem to Henry Sinclair's voyage of 1398 A.D. readers may be satisfied that the following very condensed account of the whole underground history is supported by comparable number of facts and suggestive coincidences. This is a tale that needs to be told because of the insights it can bring to an understanding of Canada's role in the past *and future* development of North America's society and politics.

If Henry Sinclair did establish a religious refuge in Nova Scotia, what happened to it?

It seems to have been relocated. The new site was Montreal.

By the middle 1500s traffic on the Atlantic was getting a bit brisk. North America was visited by Portuguese fishermen, Basque whalers, North Europeans in search of furs and no one knows who else. Any secret religious haven was becoming decidedly vulnerable to accidental, and possibly fatal, discovery. Religious wars were raging in Europe between Catholics and Protestants.

By 1600 the specific location of the refuge, Nova Scotia, became even more vulnerable because of plans for French colonization of Arcadia, as Nova Scotia was then called, and the rest of New France. Something had to be done to establish another refuge and to discourage exploration and colonization of Arcadia until this could be done. In short, a de Bouillon operative had to be infiltrated into the exploration and colonization plans for Arcadia and New France. In fact, it seems that several such infiltrators were working together to buy a bit of time for the refugees of The Cross.

The two most famous de Bouillon agents active in this particular mission were Samuel de Champlain and the Sieur de Monts. Champlain, "an ardent Catholic" so we are assured by conventional history, was a life-long friend and business partner of de Monts who was a Protestant. Further, both Champlain and de Monts had connections with the Knights of Malta, another order founded by the de Bouillon dynasty in the Holy Land.

It is thought that Champlain was born in 1587 near the old Templar port of La Rochelle, but nothing is known for certain about his birth and family. Except what he tells himself in his journals and, as recent research has shown, these are unreliable when it comes to his personal history. But Champlain does appear to be telling the truth when he says in his earliest account, the West Indies voyage of 1599, that he was sponsored in the exploration business by one Don Francisco Coloma, a Knight of Malta.

Then, the Sieur de Monts also had apparent connections with

the Knights of Malta. Nothing is known for certain about his birth or family origins either, but one document says that he was of Italian extraction. He may well have been the son of Pietro del Monte, Grand Master of the Knights of Malta during the late 1500s. But that is speculation. What is known is that this Sieur de Monts, who was frequently bankrupt because of his fur trading and colonization schemes, managed nonetheless to acquire the old Templar castle of Ardennes from . . . the Knights of Malta! De Monts, after a turbulent and somewhat curious career, came to a peaceful end in his ex-Templar castle. Unfortunately for later historians, this castle's library caught fire not long after the death of de Monts so that his memoirs, if any, have been lost.

In conventional Canadian history, Champlain and de Monts between them are credited with exploring Acadia and New France and mapping the territory (Champlain) and starting some serious attempts at colonization (de Monts). In fact, there is some evidence to suggest that they were agents of the Knights of Malta, a group who wished to establish Canada as their new base in the Americas . . . a base free from the religious persecution by the Roman Catholic church.

The eventual solution was the establishment of a new refuge at Montreal. It could not be concealed in an unknown part of the world, as Nova Scotia had been in Sinclair's day, because by the 1640s there were few habitable unexplored lands left. The new refuge was concealed under a social and religious disguise . . . it would be a religious community masquerading as orthodox Catholicism.

The Freemasons were a neo-Templar organization that grew out of Scotland with headquarters among the Sinclairs of Rosslyn. But there were several underground organizations dedicated to the de Bouillon cause, and in contact and co-operation with each other. There is evidence that the Knights of Malta were one such organization. The Illuminati of Bavaria were supposed to be another.

In the book *The Holy Blood and the Holy Grail* the authors identify a secret society in France, the Compagnie du Saint-Sacrement, as yet another underground organization working covertly for de Bouillon interests and to preserve the de Bouillon lineage.

The headquarters of the Compagnie du Saint-Sacrement were situated in the Seminary of Saint-Sulpice in Paris, a religious organization founded by Jean Jacques Olier. Although the authors of *The Holy Blood and the Holy Grail* covered only European activities of the de Bouillon underground, Canadians will immediately recall that Olier was one of the principal founders of Montreal and Canadians will remember that, somehow, the colony of Montreal came under the jurisdiction of the newly-formed Sulpicians instead of the older religious orders.

According to the traditional story forced upon conventional historians, Montreal came to be planned and established because two men who had never met each other experienced simultaneous religious visions in different French towns. One of these men was Jean Jacques Olier. The other was Jerome le Royer de la Dauversiere. They each had visions instructing them to found a hospital community on the island of Montreal in far-away New France. These two, Olier and Dauversiere, did much of the financial and personnel recruitment in France, and much of the necessary funding was contributed by a Madame de Bouillon.

It seems likely that all these people came together to found Montreal as a part of a secret conspiracy motivated by some powerful compulsion and backed by substantial resources. Careful planning, not simultaneous visions, concentrated them together according to a careful plan.

This plan called for a new refuge, away from the old Arcadian haven which was now threatened by raiders from Spain, and raids by Puritans from New England. In fact, Arcadia was attacked by Sedgwick of Massachussets in 1654.

This became the new "beach head" of the de Bouillon order in Canada, which since has spread throughout the country with the establishment of new Masonic orders and De Molay chapters.

This long "diversion" from our observations on the development of NDP philosophy is not a total digression. The establishment of the de Bouillon lineage through the Templar migrations ending in Canada, and their relevence to present day Masons and De Molay society members could have had more influence on Canadian political development than most people realize.

Perhaps now we can better appreciate the hidden meaning of that hymn that Tommy Douglas used to quote, the lines that perplexed even loyal CCF voters (not to mention Marxist fellow-travellers on Tommy's successful political bandwagon):

> I shall not cease from mortal strife,
> Nor shall my sword rest in my hand,
> Till we have built Jerusalem
> In this green and pleasant land.

This hymn, too, was a pledge to the "de Bouillon" dynasty, although, of course, the bloodline extends well beyond Godfroi de Bouillon into the mists of past and future. His name means "golden" and perhaps it was always a pseudonym. The hymn was composed by the knowledgeable poet, Blake. It describes the continuing human crusade of the ancient lineage.

No one is obligated to accept this "secret pledge" as the truth, but it is the history preserved by Templar, Freemason, Rosicrucian, Illuminati and other "neo-Templar" secret societies.

It is difficult to say how much of this underground story of Western mankind is communicated to members of orders like the Freemasons and De Molay. These organizations are like any other human constructions. Although this secret history was originally their *raison d'être,* all human organizations fossilize and calcify. What was once regarded as living truth becomes, in time, ritualized worship and behaviour devoid of meaning.

The core members of the bloodline, and their more aware and intelligent supporters, have always known this apparent truth about human psychology. They have moved on to form other groups when earlier ones have become fossilized . . . and the calcified organizations may persist for decades or years with members performing rituals and rites they no longer understand. Yet, even so, something remains alive within such organizations. . . the ideal of public service and civic commitment lingers amid the confused jumble of ritual.

This is probably the situation of the vast majority of Masonic Lodges and chapters of the Order of De Molay. Although I have presented an outline of the secret tradition that once brought these groups into being, there's no reason to believe that a young De Molay member like Tommy Douglas would have been exposed to it. He might even ridicule the notion that such a secret tradition could have been connected with his youthful De Molay chapter in any way. I do not want to suggest that Tommy Douglas was motivated by any knowledge of the perhaps fanciful history outlined.

But he was inspired by the lingering ideal of public service, civic commitment and humane progress. This ideal flourished, if only in Boy Scout fashion, within the Order of De Molay. It still does.

If this secret version of human progress is true, then it becomes obvious that supposedly "scientific" Marxism is an inadequate approximation of social development. "Methodism" becomes more valid than "Marxism", to put it into the simplistic terms of Clement Atlee, because commitment to humanistic ideals has proved a more powerful influence upon the course of history than economic materialism.

Within such a context, "Marxism" becomes merely a phase of *some* social histories in the modern world, or a sometimes useful model for designing *some* economic policies of wealth distribution, but it cannot masquerade for long as an all-embracing ideology of human inter-action.

It is more than possible that people intuitively suspect this limitation of Marxism, and it would not be surprising if they did. People of the Western World have been continuously exposed to whispers of this secret history. The underground tradition, fossilized and calcified in various ways, is even the foundation of the major Western religions. More to the point, perhaps, folk memories and myths have preserved human ideals represented by this secret history — such as chivalry — which are powerful molders of desirable behaviour. It is no accident that every hero and heroine of every book and TV drama exhibits "chivalry" and "amor courtoise". Marxism is bereft of such ideals and qualities. . . which may explain why, for instance, the OWIU leaders could propose that the Saskatchewan CCF plan of rural electrification should be scrapped so that Power Corporation could afford an across-the-board wage hike. It was not a chivalrous act.

Nonetheless, and probably because of social trends in the modern and materialist world, the CCF slowly became dominated by people motivated more by Marxism than Methodism.

The result was the transformation of the Co-operative Common-wealth Federation into the New Democratic Party.

This metamorphosis was due to the efforts of one man above all, David Lewis. There can be no doubt that Lewis created the NDP out of a profound and sincere commitment to the Marxist model for improving the world and guiding social development.

Nonetheless, it may be that David Lewis, with all the best intentions of fighting "the good fight", led the NDP down an obsolete ideological blind alley.

Chapter Four

David Lewis:

Politics of Consolidation

In describing the difference between himself and the western leaders of the CCF (Tommy Douglas, M.J. Coldwell and J.S. Woodsworth), David Lewis accurately identified the philosophical schism in the party's leadership:

> Ideologically, there was a difference in the source of one's faith, rather than the quality of one's faith. My root was the reading of Marx and Lenin (and I totally rejected communism on the basis of those writings). Their approach was moralistic.
> I looked to the Labour Party in Britain as the origin of the CCF. My memory is that M.J. and Tommy did as well, but my link was a little more alive because of my previous three years of intense work inside the (British) Labour Party. M.J. and Tommy were less convinced of the need for a labour base in Canada; they became fully convinced later.[1]

This statement by Lewis is not only an accurate appraisal of the ideological split within the CCF, but it also serves as an example of how his Marxist ideology and personality together combined to create a tendency to distort the naked truth in the interests of "ideological solidarity" as he saw it. The last sentence in the quote above is a manifestation of this tendency.

The fact of the matter was that neither M.J. Coldwell nor Tommy Douglas ever "became fully convinced" that a labour base for the CCF was needed or even desirable. Douglas was sceptical of Marxist assumptions about labour as a class in North America:

> And he rejected, as did his father, high-flown and simplistic solutions based on labour — as a class — taking power as a political power. It did not fit the Canadian experience. Douglas is dubious about the existence of genuine "solidarity" among Canadian working people. If anyone in Canada, he says, is class-conscious it is the big "middle class" with which people in many occupations identify, and which is tinged with disdain for greasy plumbers and mere manual workers. But those blue-collar workers are not proud of their class, nor loyal to it; they are individually either anxious to get out of it, or at pains to deny any distinction between their occupation and any other. They are part of the "upward mobility" syndrome of North America. Political calculation in Canada has to be careful of "class".[2]

It is difficult to account for the reason that Lewis remained convinced that Marxist and European concepts of class, and conceptions of labour as a class committed to a social struggle, were valid for Canadian society when his prominent western colleagues in the CCF had apparently abandoned this sort of Marxist dogma. It cannot be that Lewis came from a more working class or European background that the others. Douglas, and Coldwell had been born in Britain's class-conscious society, and Douglas came from definite working class origins in a Labour Party town.

David Locz ("Losh") was born in 1909 in the town of Swislocz in what was then a part of Imperial Russia. David's father was factory worker in the leather industry, and leader of the local leather workers' union. Swislocz was a typical *shtetl* with a population of about 4500 people of which about 3500 were Jewish, according to Lewis's recollections. There were once literally thousands of shtetls in Eastern Europe until they were destroyed by the Nazis and, since there is nothing quite like them in existence today, the origins of the shtetls may be of interest to readers.

In very briefly recounting the tragedies of the Jewish people in Europe, Lewis, in his memoirs, mentions in passing that the Jews were pushed "from west to east" by pogroms and discrimination. This view is what might be called the "canonical" history of the *ashkenazim*, as the Eastern European Jews are called. It has puzzled Jewish and Gentile scholars alike that, somehow, the vast majority of modern Jewry inhabited Eastern Europe. Before the Holocaust, it has been estimated by Jewish authorities that there were, perhaps, 13 million Jews in the world. Of these, about 1 million were considered *sephardim*, or Jews that could trace their origin back to Palestime due to some event in the Diaspora. But the remaining 12 million, or more than 90 per cent, lived in Eastern Europe, mostly in shtetls, and there was no known migration of the Diaspora to account for them.

Further, population analysis of known sephardic-origin Jewish communities in medieval France and Germany showed that the Jewish population was simply too small, during the Middle Ages, to result in 12 million ashkenazim by the 1930s.

A possible answer to the puzzle of the ashkenazim was supplied in 1941 by the Jewish medieval scholar, A.N. Poliak, who published an account of a very obscure historical event in his article "The Khazar Conversion to Judaism". Ten years later, Poliak expanded this article in a book, *Khazaria — The History of a Jewish Kingdom in Europe*. Poliak's work was supported, in 1962, by the work of Soviet archeologist and historian, M.I. Artamonov, who published *Khazar History* in Leningrad. But it is possible that Poliak had heard of an earlier Artamonov article on the same subject, *Studies in Ancient Khazar History*, which had been published in Leningrad in 1936. Poliak's works were published in Hebrew, and Artamonov's in Russian, and neither has been translated into English, but Hungarian-born British author, Arthur Koestler, presented the gist of their work in his 1976 book, *The Thirteenth Tribe*.[3]

It seems that a powerful south Russian nomadic tribe, the Khazars, were *converted* to Judaism about 800 A.D., or about the time that Charlemagne was crowned Holy Roman Emperor.

These Khazars were very numerous, were steppe warriors and herdsmen, and they controlled the very lucrative caravan routes between the Islamic power of Persia and the Christian "Eastern Roman Empire" of Byzantium. They felt the need for a more evolved religion than their primitive steppe shamanism, but could not adopt either Islam or Christianity without falling under the control of either Persia or Byzantium.

Being under the spiritual "tutelege" of either Persia or Byzantium, which quite obviously and inevitably meant coming under political control, did not suit Khazar political or economic ambitions. The Khazars were very happy to remain the balance of power and artery of commerce, between these two waring religious empires. Some Khazar political genius hit upon the idea of choosing Judaism instead of either Islam or Christianity. This gave the Khazars, at one stroke, a religion as venerable than either Islam or Christianity, one that was, moreover, the origin of both, but also independent and different from both.

The Khazars were converted *en masse*, and there were hundreds of thousands of them even in the 9th Century, and they prospered for another 300 or 400 years. It may be difficult to imagine, but it is nonetheless a historical fact, that a very powerful Jewish Kingdom controlled much of southern Russia from about 800 A.D. until about 1200 A.D. It was a Hebrew-speaking kingdom, because the language had been introduced along with the religion, and the existence and power of Khazaria is attested by the numerous archeological finds of Hebrew coinage.

But Khazaria, like much else, was swept away by the Mongol invasions of the 13th Century. Khazar refugees, along with a mixed bag of other refugees, including Goths and Magyars, were pushed relentlessly westward by the Mongols and ended up where the ashkenazim lived until Hitler all but eliminated them in the Holocaust. The Magyars, now living in Hungary, were originally steppe neighbors of these Khazars when they all lived around the Caspian, or The Khazar Sea as it was then called.

The Khazar remnants, then, ending up in what is now called Eastern Europe, became the ashkenazim and nicely accounted for the otherwise inexplicable 12 million Jews inhabiting the area as of about 1930.

Shtetls were nothing more or less than mixed farming/ranching settlements on the Khazar steppe model. Much of what we assume to be Jewish culture is, in fact, not "Jewish" at all, but is simply steppe culture preserved by the ashkenazim descendants of the Khazars. As Koestler (among others) points out, the sort of kaftan worn by Orthodox Eastern European rabbis, and the fur-trimmed flat hat of distinctive shape, both originated as steppe garments worn alike by Khazars and other tribes. Even the traditional Jewish dish, *gefillte fisch* seems to be of steppe, and not Palestinian origin, deriving from a Khazar method of preparing sturgeon from The Khazar Sea.

Needless to say, the "Khazar connection" raises some profound questions which are not only well beyond the subject of this book, but which present everyone with disturbing ironies ... and yet, the "Khazar connection" provides another example of comfortable and conventional history revealed as much less than the truth, a distortion fuelling much unnecessary conflict and suffering.

We are accustomed to think of Eastern European Jews as urban ghetto-dwellers and, very possibly, by 1930 perhaps the majority of ashkenazim did live in sections of major East European cities. But it is also possible that the majority, or a significant minority, lived in the shtetls. These were small and friendly market towns, with a very predominant and cohesive Jewish culture. The shtetls were dotted throughout the country-side and served the needs of the countryfolk by being places where garden produce and livestock might be sold by sur-rounding Jewish farmers and ranchers, and where these farmers and ranchers could obtain necessary goods from the shtetl crafts-men and merchants. Except for the language, *Yiddish,* a refugee patois of mixed Hebrew, Slavonic and Gothic linguistic elements, and except for the predominant religion, Judaism, life in the shtetls was much like life anywhere else in agrarian Europe up to the 1900s.

It is now usual to think of Jews as urban professionals and businessmen, but in the East European shtetls they were acknow-ledged as expert farmers, livestock breeders, horsemen and wagon-makers ... or, in short, exactly what the Khazars had been long before. The Jewish monopoly and know-how in the crucial art of wagon-making was so all-pervasive in Eastern Europe that the modern Russian word for wagoneer, *balagula,* comes from the Hebrew *ba'al agalah.*

In the town of Swizlocz, therefore, young David Locz was born into a very confident and cohesive Jewish culture, a rural market-town, and experienced in his youngest years little or no "anti-Semitism" for the simple reason that the town was over-whelmingly Jewish.

Nonetheless, there was a great deal of conflict among the town's population which could have been a source of confusion for young David Locz.

While David Lewis's memoirs contain no recollection of violence or discrimination is Swizlocz itself during his very young years before the First World War, the Jewish community was continually aware of the danger of pogroms which swept through shtetl country with monotonous and tragic regularity. Hundreds or thousands of Jews were massacred annually — no one will ever know how many — in these obscure towns when outsiders in-vaded for the purpose of killing and raping. Jews in the urban ghettos experienced the same horror year after year.

Within the Jewish community as a whole there were two more or less opposite strategies for a solution, and they were formed about the same time. Each gained numerous adherents.

One strategy was the development of Zionism, the idea that Jews would never be safe until they possessed a country of their own. The obvious country was part of Palestine, the promised land of the Bible and the Jews' supposed homeland. Zionism attracted many followers, collected money to purchase parcels of land in the Holy Land, and in the fullness of time resulted in the modern state of Israel.

A completely opposite tack was represented by the Jewish Workers' Bund ("Alliance") which, as the name itself suggests, was Marxist-socialist in nature and composed mostly of factory and unionized workers. The ideology of the Bund was built on the premise that only a minority of Jews could ever hope to emigrate to a Jewish state in the promised land (if one were ever established, which, in the early 1900s, seemed unlikely). The only real solution for Jews was to change society so that senseless discrimination no longer existed. It was the Marxist view that discrimination and aggression were the result of nationalism and capitalism and, if both could be abolished through the triumph of internationlist socialism, then discrimination against Jews would cease automatically. While the concern of the Jewish Workers' Bund was oriented toward the plight of Jews in particular, its ideology was much broader. They were concerned with the plight of all people who suffered the effects of nationalism and capitalism, not just Jews.

In line with the tenets of Marxism, Bundists were necessarily anti-religious. For them, religion was just another mechanism, like nationalism and capitalism, which divided people artificially and with dangerous emotion, into differing groups exhibiting xenophobia and chauvinism. For Bundists, whether from a Jewish origin or not, Judaism as a religion, and the ideal of "Israel" as a national state, both contributed to the very sort of society that resulted in pogroms.

As may be easily imagined, the schism between the Zionists and Bundists cut deepy into the Jewish communities of Eastern Europe where emotion was already at a level of near-hysteria due to the almost daily news of massacres in neighboring towns. While one half of the population took the "Next year in Jerusalem" vow very seriously indeed, the other half of the population was not only questioning the justification for "Israel", but questioning the righteousness of Judaism.

It was a confrontation that could, and did, divide families. The Locz family was right in the middle of this storm of Jewish soul-searching. David's father had become a Marxist, an agnostic, and an active leader in the leather workers' union and the Jewish Workers' Bund. *His* father, on the other hand, was a prominent mill-owner, a non-Marxist and a devout Jew.

Swislocz was occupied by the German army during World War I and, during the taking of the town, the Locz sheltered along with many others in an over-crowded cellar. The spectre of combat and bodies of dead soldiers that littered Swislocz's streets made a lasting impression on young David.

As in the home of Tommy Douglas, political discussion was an integral part of the Locz family activities. Being a leader of unionized workers and of the Bund, David's father hosted many guests for political discussion and organization. David was fascinated, from the first, in politics and socialism as interpreted by his father and the Bund activists. The Locz family was pleased, initially, at the news of the Russian Revolution and the overthrow of Czarism ... but somewhat less than pleased when the Bolsheviks took control from the Mensheviks. The Locz family, although detesting Czarism and all it stood for, were nonetheless democratic socialists. While cheering the revolution on one hand, they were also wary of the revolutionaries. And this distrust was daily augmented by stories of shtetl refugees fleeing from Russia with tales of Bolshevik terrorism. David's family was to experience this terrorism first-hand.

After World War I, Poland was reconstituted and the town of Swislocz found itself relocated inside the new Polish frontier instead of inside Russia. By 1919, the 'Western Allies had decided to try to reverse the Russian Revolution by engaging in war against the Soviet state through a series of muddled, incompetent and unco-ordinated invasions by expeditionary forces of various nations. Eventually, no less that 15 nations contributed soldiers in a fruitless attempt to bring down the new regime in alliance with the White Russian loyalists who, in theory, were at least mostly Czarist or in favour of a truly democratic Russian republic.

The White armies proved to be no more effective than the former Czarist ones, and the expeditionary forces of participating nations provided a comic opera of military mismanagement.

In a word, the allies were no match for the new Red Army commanded by a school teacher named Leon Trotsky.

The newly reconstituted country of Poland was chivvied into the anti-Bolshevik campaign by Britain and the United States . . . and promptly found itself invaded by the Red Army. The Bolsheviks captured Swislocz, considered the Bund to be "counter-revolutionary" and imprisoned David's father with the intention of shooting him in short order. A petition by townsfolk, and some angry demonstrations, saved the elder Locz from summary execution, but not without a time of intense fear on the part of David and the family. From that time onward, David hated the communists . . . and feared them.

David had an uncle, Eli, who had emigrated to Canada at the turn of the century. After the experience of the First World War, the Red Army's invasion of Swislocz, plus the fact that the new Polish government was exhibiting both anti-democratic and anti-Semitic symptoms, David's father looked at the situation coldly and decided that Swislocz could not offer much of a future to his family. Accordingly, he decided with his brother to emigrate to Canada. In May 1921 they left Poland for Canada and arrived in Montreal where they got jobs in the uncle's textile factory. They worked hard and saved money so that in just four months the Locz family back in Swislocz received third-class railway tickets and steerage steamship passages. David, his mother, a sister and brother, and an aunt came to Canada, landing in Montreal in August 1921.

No one spoke a word of English, or French, upon arrival, except what David's father had been able to pick up in the four months he'd worked in Montreal.

But Montreal seemed a wonderland to David. He had never been in a large city before. Even the very modest working-class flat that sheltered the family was luxury after the shtetl. On their first evening in their new home, the Locz children flicked the electric lights off and on and begged to be able to light the elements of the gas stove. They had never seen such things in Poland.

At first, school was a terrible ordeal for the children, but especially for Daivd, In Poland, he had been a very good student, but in Montreal he could not even speak the language. He was placed in the first grade with six-year-olds even though he was thirteen. And he could not even understand the simplest question the teacher might ask, much less answer it. Naturally, the other youngsters laughed at him. David pleaded with his father that he might be allowed to find a job, learn English in his spare time, and then return to school when he could at least speak the language. But his father would have none of it, knowing that confronting the school problem without delay was David's best hope of future fulfillment.

David was determined to make up for lost time. He bought a copy of *The Old Curiosity Shop* by Charles Dickens and a Yiddish-English dictionary. He taught himself English word-by-word within a few months. Inside of a year he had a better English vocubulary than many of his native-born schoolmates and he worked after school with sympathetic teachers on his pronumciation. He began to skip grades very quickly so that by 1924 he entered Baron Byng High School, and he skipped two grades there to graduate with his proper age group in 1926. In addition to his schooling, David worked constantly in order to assist his family and to put something aside so that he could go on to attend university.

Early on, David's father had decided to change the family name. "Lewis" was decided on as a fair approximation of Locz as pronounced in Polish. This name, together with the "slight lilt" in David's speech (due to very hurried lessons in pronunciation) caused him, in later life, to be frequently mistaken for a Welshman! This misapprehension became a source for later campaign humour.

It was a girl, naturally, that spurred David Lewis to skip two grades in High School. Her name was Sophie Carson and, once falling in love with her, Lewis decided never to let her go. She, however, was in her graduating year when David was only in the second year. This bothered him a great deal, because he wanted to graduate with her. With the faith and assistance of a sympathetic Principal, who had reason to be impressed with David's academic abilities, he did so. David and Sophie were inseparable thereafter.

The Lewis family remained active in politics and union affairs in Canada, just as it had been in Swislocz. David's father joined the Amalgamated Clothing Workers of America and engaged in spirited political discussions with friends and fellow-workers as before. But they had to adjust to some cultural differences ...

> My father and Uncle Max had soon become members of their respective local unions of the Amalgamated Clothing Workers of America and were becoming adjusted to the attitudes and policies of Canadian unions. They found them much less concerned with building a socialist society but more effective in winning concessions for the members. So I heard my father argue on a number of occasions with friends who gathered in our home in Montreal, as friends had done in Swislocz. What was conveyed to me was joy at having come to Canada and great hopes for the future, especially for the children. The labour movement was not class-conscious or militant, but conditions of work were immeasurably better. My father, always logical, argued that it was necessary to adjust politically and culturally to the new environment and not to live nostalgically back in the shtetl.[4]

Personally, I find something at once significant and rather poignant about this paragraph from David Lewis's memoirs, and we will return to it later as part of an assessment of what Lewis accomplished with the New Democratic Party.

David Lewis was a busy young man from the instant he landed in Montreal in 1921, but there may also have been an element of culture-shock and timidity when he admits that ...

> Two or three years passed before I saw the wealthy homes of Outremont and I did not walk the posh streets of Westmount until I entered university in 1927.[5]

For his first six years in Canada, David Lewis stayed within the familiar Yiddish-speaking Jewish immigrant area centred on St. Urbain Street, later made famous, as Lewis remarked, "thanks to the writings of Mordecai Richler".

But if Lewis was in something of a protective cultural shell while he learned English in school and French on the streets, he came out of it with a vengeance when he entered McGill University. He became a prolific joiner of all the university clubs going. Lewis remembered his college days as the start of a 50-year political career. He joined various trade union organizations and

also the League for Social Reconstruction because of his associations with Eugene Forsey, King Gordon, Frank Scott, the
University of Toronto's Frank Underhill and J.S. Woodsworth
... all of whom were destined to become prominent personalities
in the Co-operative Commonwealth Federation. Lewis was also
active in the Student Christian Movement which was, at that
time, an organization embracing rather radical "socialist-
Christian" ideals not too dissmiliar from the message being
played simultaneously by Tommy Douglas on his bull fiddie out
in Weyburn, Saskatchewan.

Unlike Douglas, however, Lewis's direct involvement in
Canadian politics was postponed for a few years by a somewhat
remarkable twist of fate which even Lewis found extremely
puzzling. After graduating with a Bachelor of Arts in 1931, Lewis
entered the McGill Law School in the fall of the same year.

> One day in October or November, Colonel Bovey
> stopped me in the halls and said, completely out of the blue,
> "David, you should apply for a Rhodes Scholarship." My
> expression went blank. I had never heard of the Rhodes
> Scholarships and told him so. He explained them briefly to
> me and suggested where I could get more information... he
> urged me to follow it up and offered himself as one of my
> sponsors. After some investigation, I concluded that Bovey
> was just being kind. Aside from any other consideration, I
> had not taken part in any athletic activity, and this was, as I
> understood the literature, one of the three main
> requirements for the scholarship. Indeed, even my
> scholastic record was not overwhelming.[6]

Lewis was even more puzzled when Professor Frank Scott
made the same suggestion "quite independently". Lewis applied,
although he could not see how an avowed socialist and a jew, not
to mention a non-athlete without an exceptional academic record
as an undergraduate, could hope to win.

Nonetheless, much to his own amazement and to the delight of
his parents, he did win the coveted scholarship which meant an
opportunity to study law at Oxford with ample funds.

> The prize itself was a great honour, but to win it in 1932
> was doubly fortuitous. I was in first-year law and was
> beginning to worry about the financial situation; it was

becoming increasingly difficult to find part-time and summer jobs as the Depression deepened.

I immediately insisted that Sophie should come to England with me. The scholarship did not permit me to marry, but I could see no reason why we should not share together the adventure of three years across the Atlantic.[7]

As strange as it may seem for the times, Sophie's very Orthodox family of a seriously ill father and brothers (her mother having died some years before) did agree to her going to England with David. There was even enough money in the scholarship for them to take a side-trip to Swislocz before they settled in England. The beautiful and sweet Sophie easily passed family muster as David's fiancée among the concerned relatives of Swislocz. David and Sophie were both appalled by the poverty of his home town during the Depression, but it was lucky that Sophie and David visited Swislocz when they did because the war to come not only obliterated David's birthplace, but also David's relatives in the town. In 1978, three years after Ed Broadbent became leader of the NDP, Lewis and a friend travelled back to Swislocz which had reverted to being in Soviety territory. Lewis remembered:

> In May 1978, in company with a friend, I travelled to the Soviet Union to revisit Swislocz, his birthplace and mine. Today it lies a few kilometres east of the Polish border in the Soviet Republic of Byelorussia. The visit proved to be a disturbing experience, for we could not recognize any part of the town; the Nazis and the Second World War had completely obliterated our past. I stood in the centre of a new, well-planned town and remembered with pain and nostalgia the Swislocz of my boyhood . . .[8]

In 1932, some 46 years earlier, he and Sophie were in their early twenties, with all of life before them, and in spite of the depressing realities of Depression Swislocz, they knew they had a different future from the one about to confront David's Polish relations.

In order to get to Swislocz in Poland in 1932, they had to pass through Hitler's new Germany by rail. In his memoirs, Lewis gives a very brief and conventional account of his impressions of this Germany which would erase his roots in the few years to come. He says only, and in a paragraph that begins with his arrival in London and meeting a "much-loved friend", the following about passing through Nazi Germany on his way to his home town:

> The train trip was fascinating but disturbing. The German newspapers were filled with stories of violent clashes between roving Nazi bands and groups of socialists and communists. I had not realized the gravity of the Hitler threat and was astonished and frightened by what I read while in Germany.[9]

Considering the fact that David Lewis's memoirs of this period were published in 1981 with plenty of opportunity to modify recollections with the benefit of hindsight, this must rank as a most astonishingly mild judgment of 1932 Germany by someone who was not only a professed socialist but also a Jew. A near-contemporary, John F. Kennedy, who travelled through Germany at about the same time, and who was neither a professed socialist nor a Jew, was so disturbed at what he witnessed that he felt obligated to write a lengthy book on the subject, *While England Slept*. This effort, Kennedy admitted, was not a very good book, but it was created by a young man who was worried enough to extend his "grand tour" type of European holiday in an effort to observe more about the Nazi phenomenon.

One gets the impression that Lewis was capable of closing his eyes, or focusing them stolidly upon Sophie, in order to record so little of a personal trip through 1932 Germany ... especially as a would-be leader of a socialist party in Canada and as a Jew.

And, in fact, one finds that his personal and first-hand observations of Nazi-leaning Germany are limited to these few words, while his descriptions of Sir Stafford Cripps's estate in England, and descriptions of Lady Cripps's "graciousness" are dealt with at greater length. And all this curious emphasis in a chapter bravely entitled "A Socialist at Oxford". With the brief references to Nazis and the longer account of his and Sophie's painful visit to Swislocz taken care of at the start of this chapter of his memoirs, Lewis devotes great space to what really occupied his mind in those years — the intellectual excitement of Oxford and his associations with leading lights in the British Labour Party.

David and Sophie were met in London by Jennie Lee, a British Labour M.P. who'd been elected to British Parliament in 1929 and who had been a guest speaker in Montreal when Lewis was attending McGill. Lee was able to introduce David and Sophie to the prominent Labour leaders of the day, David was naturally interested in finding out more about the British Labour Party because of its possible relevance to the Canadian political scene. It may be significant that David not only looked to the British Labour Party as a "parent" to the colonial social democratic movement in Canada, but he also gravitated immediately toward the establishment mainstream of that party. His view of radicals is worth quoting at some length because of its relevance to his later reaction to the so-called "Waffles" within the NDP:

> One of the earliest socialist organizations in Britain was the Independent Labour Party (ILP), founded in 1893 by Keir Hardie, a legendary figure in the country's labour movement. The ILP played an active role in the formation of the Labour Party and became affiliated with it, acting as its socialist conscience. However, in 1932 a majority voted to disaffiliate from the Labour Party because of differences of ideology and policy. Jimmy Maxton and Fenner Brockway, the two leading spokesmen for the ILP at the time, were men of principle and integrity. I had the good fortune to meet them both more than once and was captivated by their oratory and personal charm. But their explanation of what they expected to accomplish by leaving the Labour Party was unconvincing. ... I was almost impolite in my lack of sympathy. Separate, purist, splinter groups never appealed to me, even in my earliest years of socialist activity. The exclusiveness of such groups always seemed to me self-indulgent futility and even recklessness, for the objectives of democratic socialism can only be achieved by a united mass party.[10]

While it is quite obviously true that any political party, if it is to be effective, must maintain a certain degree of solidarity it is important to ensure that the party as a whole is founded upon the major source of populist support. David Lewis persisted in viewing the British Labour Party as an organization built upon militant labour as a class and build upon Marxism as a guiding ideology. Why he persisted in this will be dealt with later when we come to what can only be called "parlour psychiatry" in an effort to explain his motivations. In viewing the British Labour Party it is clear that David Lewis saw it through eyes that were focused during his lost Swislocz boyhood. He did not see the British Labour Party as it really was, but as a wholly Marxist-labour creation ... similar, perhaps, to the Bund of his father. Lewis didn't seriously consider the truth of Atlee's statement that even the British Labour Party owed "more to Methodism than to Marx".

It is odd that Lewis could consider the ILP a "splinter group" when he himself correctly described it as an organization that "played an active role in the formation of the British Labour Party". Possibly it was because he had a need of security, meaning "establishment" and the imposition of order ... all dominated by automatic and unexamined Marxist assumptions.

It may also be symptomatic of Lewis's psychological needs that he automatically assumed that the British Labour Party must have been, or should be, the parental role model for the democratic socialist movement in Canada when he stated ...

"I looked to the Labour Party in Britain as the origin of the CCF."

As we have seen, this assumption on Lewis's part was in error. The CCF grew out of a meeting between Coldwell and Douglas at the suggestion of Woodsworth . . . who where all thoroughly familiar with the Canadian realities on the prairies. And, as we have seen, the CCF, was not primarily a labour party at all, but was more a farmers' party in terms of voter support and only secondarily a coalition with organized labour. Further, one of the principal elected spokesmen of the CCF, Tommy Douglas, thought and acted from a purely Canadian perspective and on several occasions criticized the British habit of making pater-nalistic and colonial assumptions about Canada.

In spite of all this, Lewis needed to believe that Canada's CCF was a child of the British Labour Party, just as he needed to believe that even the British Labour Party was a wholly Marxist and class-conscious construction. The truth was that the British Labour Party, while being more of a Marxist and class-conscious worker construct than the CCF ever was, was not quite so wholly constructed as Lewis apparently needed to believe.

It is not surprising that Lewis enjoyed his Oxford education and his associations with the established British Labour Party immensely. He mentions the famous people that he met: Stafford Cripps, Harold Laski, G.D.H. Cole, Nye Bevan, William Mellor, Ellen Wilkinson and Barbara Castle. He had Sophie enjoyed some weekend visits on the estate of Sir Stafford and Lady Cripps. There was the Devon holiday with the young American writer, Paul Engle, and the British poet, C. Day Lewis. There was the summer of 1933 spent in the Chateau district of France. He and Sophie appreciated the artistic entertainment that London offered:

> For obvious reasons I have emphasized my political and trade-union contacts, but Sophie's and my interests were always wider. London's wealth of plays, opera, dance and music lured us to the least expensive seats of a theatre every evening we were not otherwise occupied. At Oxford I listened to and met visiting writers, particularly poets ..."

In 1934 David and Sophie vacationed on the continent, this time travelling through the fascist countries. Although Lewis devotes a number of pages of his memoirs to this 1934 view of Nazi-land (much more than his brief observations of the 1932 trip through Germany), there is clearly an avoidance of the whole impleasant situation. Lewis does not appear to have objectively assessed the urgent threat of Naziism, but instead, he seems to have viewed the growing storm in Europe with some sense of intellectual and historical detachment. In a Vienna "more than halfway to the *Anschluss*", it was not the immediate and clear menace of Naziism that induced philosophical speculations, but the larger scope of human history ... with Marxist over-tones.

> Despite the sadness which filled our stay in Vienna, we could not ignore the grace and charm of the city. It had been the seat of emperors and had the legacy of monuments in architecture, castles and gardens, churches and statues, which kings leave behind them. The artistry left one breathless. Yet I could not avoid asking myself, as I had done in Warsaw, Paris and London, Rome and Florence,

whether this great cultural wealth was worth the price in human suffering and human lives which it had cost through the centuries. It posed a moral question which I was not then, and have never been, able to answer.[12]

Lewis was as amused as he was depressed by Nazi racist double-talk, and he clipped the following advertisement from a Vienna newspaper and sent it to his parents in Yiddish translation:

The blond ladies with the milk-white colour of their faces, who have nothing in common with the Jewish race, suffer sunburn. The ordinary beauty creams, which are adequate for the common, black skin of the Semites, cannot be suitable for the gentle softness of the German shades of colour.
There is a Japanese product, an ideal cream, wonderful for the Aryan skin. Thus, recognizing the greatness of the Nordic races, do the yellow peoples of the distant Orient take care of the model Aryan race. Long live Hitler![13]

David and Sophie, depressed by their 1934 venture through fascist Germany, Italy and Austria, were happy to get back to Britain.

Lewis made his mark at Oxford, not only because of his academic achievements, but also because of his social and political activities at the university. In his final year, Lewis became President of the Oxford Union, a singular honour for a "colonial". A weekly student magazine, *Isis*, describes the impression that Lewis had had on his fellow students:

When David Lewis steps into the Union Presidency next term, he will be, beyond question, the least Oxonian person ever to lead to the Society. In appearance, background and intellectual outlook he is a grim antithesis to all the suave, slightly delicate young men who for generations have sat on the Union rostrum ...
The almost ferocious energy with which Lewis defends his convictions is, however, the root of his most dangerous fault. Tolerance comes hard. He cannot help attacking hypocrisy, snobbery and muddled thinking with a scathing, merciless sarcasm. His forthright earnestness has antagonized many of the more timid and soft-spoken Oxonians. At the same time it has won their respect.[14]

Lewis won the respect of the British Labour Party, too, and of important trade union organizations. Just before returning to Canada in the summer of 1935, Lewis had to struggle with "a serious temptation to remain in England". David was offered a safe Labour seat in the upcoming British elections and Sir Stafford Cripps offered him a lawyer's job in his legal office. Lewis described his temptations:

> ... A political future, my major interest, was assured. Within months I would almost certainly be a Member of Parliament and within a few years, part of a Labour government in one role or another. At the same time, I didn't know exactly what I would do professionally in Canada, particularly since we would return penniless. And politically there was a long, hard road ahead, since the CCF was just getting off the ground.[15]

Since he was only human, it may be imagined that David Lewis often had reason to regret his own sense of commitment that compelled him to return to Canada in 1935. There is little doubt that he would have achieved very great success within the British Labour Party and it is not at all beyond the realm of possibility that he might have become Prime Minister. Certainly, at the very least, he would have attained a more comfortable level of financial security for his family. Further, as he admitted freely, "Sophie and I loved London, and the English people ..." and "Sophie and I discussed the matter earnestly for days".

But David and Sophie decided, after all, to return to the political and professional uncertainties of Canada:

> I cannot say what influenced me most; human motives are never simple. Undoubtedly the fact that Sophie's family and my own were in Montreal played a part. Also important was the fact that throughout my three years at Oxford I had been preparing myself to help build a social democratic movement in Canada, not elsewhere. I felt a deep gratitude to Canada for the opportunities which had opened up before me almost from the day I first arrived in Montreal fourteen years earlier. Canada was my country.[16]

While at Oxford, David had kept abreast of political developments at home. He and Woodsworth had corresponded, and

David had received an account of the preliminary Calgary meeting of 1932 and then a copy of the resultant Regina Manifesto adopted at the CCF founding convention in 1933. Woodsworth continued to correspond with David, gently recruiting him for the CCF, but (as always) refusing to paint a rosy picture of the future. In a letter received shortly after David finally decided to return to Canada, Woodsworth contrasted what the CCF could offer as against what had already been tendered by the British Labour Party:

> At a little meeting of the LSR (League for Social Reconstruction) of Montreal, we were discussing the situation at this coming election, and someone suggested that you might possible be free. We were all unanimous that if this were the case, there was a wonderful field for your activities here in Canada. I had heard the rumour some time ago that you might enter public life in Great Britain, and I can well understand the openings that there would be there, but if you have any pull in the direction of Canada, we can assure you plenty of hard work and more or less uncertainty, but at the same time, a great opportunity to wake up and organize this young country of ours.[17]

Missives like this one from Woodsworth, plus his own sense of responsibility, left David Lewis with no option but to regretfully decline the British offers and to face up to decades of struggle and disappointment in his adopted land. He and Sophie arrived back in Montreal in early August 1935, but it was a homecoming "tinged with sadness and some anxiety" because of the uncertain future they faced. But one thing had long ago been decided upon, and that was their determination to face it together. Now that David's formal education was behind him and marriage no longer forbidden by the Rhodes Scholarship which had sustained them in England, he and Sophie married immediately (on August 15, 1935, less than two weeks after their arrival in Montreal).

After a brief honeymoon in the Laurentians, David returned to Montreal to find a waiting letter from an Ottawa law firm which had had some legal interaction with Sir Stafford Cripps's law firm during the summer. Sir Stafford had mentioned Lewis to his Canadian associate. Lewis travelled immediately to Ottawa and was cordially invited to sign aboard the law firm of Russell Smart (Smart and Biggar), a legal office specializing in patents, trademarks and copyrights, at a salary of $75 a month to start.

About the same time, Lewis received another letter from Woodsworth who had been assured that young David was, indeed, coming back to Canada in spite of British blandishments. In this letter of August, Woodsworth outlined the CCF's situation for the upcoming federal election of 1935 ... the party was destitute ... and a candidate ...

> ... must either finance himself or, like invading armies of old, live on the people it conquers ... This may all seem like making bricks without straw — but somehow the bricks are actually being made! ... We are in the position where a man must show his qualities of leadership by leading, by drumming up a group and gradually securing support ... we need in the worst way the services you could give and your help in Parliament would be invaluable ... I'm afraid that this is all very indefinite but for me life has been rather indefinite and yet things have worked and so I suppose one gets into the habit of relying upon hidden opportunities ahead — as in a fog each step opens up the step ahead.[18]

This sort of thing could not have seemed particularly encouraging to David Lewis or any other potential candidate. Besides, by the time David and Sophie had found a small apartment in Ottawa and settled in, there was no time to consider a campaign for the 1935 election which was held on October 8, or only about nine weeks after David's arrival back in Canada. He was not even fully familiar with the issues or with the details of the CCF platform.

Shortly after the election, a historic event of sorts occurred in the annals of the CCF and the NDP. After the election, David went up to Parliament Hill to meet Woodsworth, congratulate him, and make the acquaintance of other CCF Members who'd won a seat. There were only eight of them, five from the prairies, one of whom was Tommy Douglas. It was at this meeting that Woodsworth made a suggestion that was to symbolize the tensions within the CCF and NDP leadership for many years to come. Since David Lewis had not run in the 1935 election, Woodsworth offered him another type of party job. Turning suddenly to Lewis, he said:

You know, Mr. Lewis, Mr. Coldwell is now not only a Member of Parliament, he is also the national secretary-treasurer of the CCF. I'm worried that this will be too much for one person. Could you perhaps find the time to help him in his duties as movement secretary? That would be a really useful contribution.[19]

Lewis recalled his response:

Without hesitation I said yes. I knew, of course, that the work would be voluntary but I also knew that Sophie, who had decided to have a family as soon as possible rather than look for a job, would be happy to help. Thus my involvement with the CCF at the national centre began within months of my return from Oxford.[20]

I have emphasized Lewis' description of his involvement — *at the national centre* — because, I think, these words betray a misapprehension on the part of David Lewis, a flaw in his perspective that was to plague the CCF-NDP. In fact, it can be said that the legacy of his misapprehension persists today and has infected the modern NDP with a sort of chronic disease.

Woodsworth's offer to Lewis began the subtle tug-of-war between Tommy Douglas, and other CCFers who had been elected, and those eastern organizers and philosophers who did not represent the "grassroots" CCF electorate. The fact of the matter was that "the national centre" of the CCF was only geographically situated in the east and Ottawa simply because that's where Parliament happened to be located. The fact that party bureaucrats, like Lewis, operated in the "national centre" of Ottawa was a purely historical and geographical accident having nothing whatever to do with the real national centre of the CCF as a political party, movement or expression.

That centre, the geographical and emotional heartland which produced the great majority of CCF Members of Parliament, was the prairies ... a region that David Lewis had never even visited. Saskatchewan was as unknown to David Lewis as the dark side of the moon ... and about as relevant to his preconceptions of what makes a social democratic party.

I think it is relevant also that Lewis juxtaposed his involvement "at the national centre" with his Oxford experience in the same sentence. Fresh from his associations with the very successful British Labour Party, which Lewis considered to be the parent of the CCF, it was perhaps natural that he'd assume that he understood what the CCF was all about. Britain, of course, represented an entirely different social and geographical situation.

Woodsworth's spontaneous offer to Lewis, which was quickly accepted, began the conflict between the unelected "centrist" bureaucrats and thinkers in the east and the CCF's actual elected representatives from the west. It seems that Woodsworth was not aware of Lewis's profound misapprehensions about the true nature of the CCF and ignorant of Lewis's reverence for the British Labour Party. Woodsworth was certainly innocent of any inkling of the tragic repercussions of his offer to David Lewis. He himself had no illusions about the nature of the CCF and no particular reverence for the established British Labour Party. As he said in Regina at the 1933 CCF founding convention:

> Perhaps it is because I am a Canadian of several genera-
> tions, and have inherited the individualism common to all
> born on the American continent; yet with political and
> social ideals profoundly influenced by British traditions and
> so-called Christian idealism . . . I am convinced that we may
> develop in Canada a distinctive type of Socialism. I refuse to
> follow slavishly the British model or the American model or
> the Russian model. We in Canada will solve our own
> problems along our own lines.[21]

Unfortunately, Woodsworth's own spontaneous offer to David Lewis was to betray the sentiments of his Regina address to the CCF convention. Unelected, but in important bureaucratic capacities, David Lewis was to impose upon the CCF and NDP organizational "solidarity" similar to what he admired among the establishment leaders of the British Labour Party. He was to impose a Marxist ideological solidarity on party policy and philosophy that was similar to the Bund of his boyhood.

In the most ironic manner, David Lewis was to head what he feared . . . *a splinter group* . . . although he would never see it that way. The mainstream of any political party must be those policies, personalities and philosophies which produce electoral success. For the CCF this quite obviously meant the Christian-ideal prairie populism represented by people like Douglas, who got elected. Within the Canadian reality, and the CCF's true political reality, David Lewis actually represented a Marxist-oriented splinter group. But he considered his outlook to be the mainstream, and considered the prairie moralists to be quaintly irrelevant to the larger purposes of the "Movement"... in spite of the electoral results. Unfortunately for the CCF and NDP as political parties, David Lewis found himself in national organizational roles which allowed him to mold them according to his splinter-group preconceptions.

* * * * * *

Lewis began working immediately for Coldwell on a part-time and volunteer (unpaid) basis as a sort of all 'round assistant secretary in national CCF affairs. On August 6, 1936 Lewis's title of National Secretary of the party was made official, although he was still labouring for the CCF without pay. Two years later, in 1938, it seemed obvious to everyone that the CCF needed a full-time National Secretary. After some further soul-searching with Sophie, sharpened by his increased responsibilities as a father because the first son, Stephen, had been born on November 11, 1937, David decided that serving the CCF was more important than establishing his legal career. Accordingly, in 1938 he resigned from the firm of Russell and Biggar and accepted the position of paid National Secretary with the party.

The financial problem entailed in this move, for David Lewis personally, was that he'd have to raise his own salary somehow. The CCF did not initially have the funds to pay him.

Lewis had not expected much in the way of organization when he became involved in the party in 1936, but what he immediately confronted was far below even his minimal expectations. The Co-operative Commonwealth Federation was exactly that — a federation of autonomous farm and labour groups, and provincial organizations, that had mutually decided to come together for political purposes, under the CCF banner. But all the groups were independent in both theory and practice, while sharing (with much disagreement on details) a social democratic philosophy sheltered under the CCF umbrella. The CCF was never a party in the sense that the Liberals and Conservatives were political parties — it was a coalition of like-minded groups. There was no such thing as a "national membership" in the CCF, and the national organization of the party, insofar as it could be said to exist, depended upon what the affiliated groups and organizations chose to donate to the national centre's treasury. The CCF's money came from membership dues collected by the various independent affiliates or from spontaneous donations from private individuals, and a portion of this income was forwarded to Ottawa for the operation of the national party. Since the CCF's natural constituency was improverished, the income at the grassroots collection level was comically small compared to what the Liberals and Tories enjoyed because of corporate donations. Only a small percentage of this tiny income was passed on to the "national CCF", because the local organizations needed some of the money for their own operations.

Lewis outlined the situation as he found it in 1936.

> The national treasury was empty, there was no national secretariat and no national office until the fall of 1936, and even then the "office" we enjoyed was, as I shall describe later, as unusual as it was uncomfortable. Across the whole of our vast country there were no more than about half a dozen full-time workers, and they had no funds with which to function effectively. There was one national organizer in the person of Ted Garland, a splendid orator with a voice as mellifluous as that of a Shakespearian actor. But poor Garland had to travel back and forth across the country by train, usually sitting up nights in a coach seat for lack of money to buy a berth, and spending much of his time raising his own expenses and a meagre salary of one hundred dollars a month.[22]

Although some of the party's unelected leaders and thinkers were well aware that the CCF could not hope to become a national force in Canadian politics under these sorts of circumstances, the elected CCF representatives themselves did not seem so concerned. Frank Underhill, who had drafted much of the Regina Manifesto for the CCF, wrote urgently to Woodsworth:

> I do feel very strongly that the movement must advance

beyond the stage of being a collection of individual missionaries and must get more organization and more conscious direction at the centre.[23]

But Woodsworth replied ...

We simply have to cut our coat according to our cloth. We have not had the finances ... most of us have been working to the very limit of our physical and nervous strength ... I really think that you hardly realize how weak we are throughout the country and how essential individual mission work is at the present time.[24]

On an earlier occasion he had expressed the same sort of sentiments to another critic of the party's national organization:

... but if this is a genuine peoples' movement, it seems to me that the people, themselves, all over the country, will have to take the matter up in their own localities. All we can do is to give a lead, then we must trust that there will come to the front individuals and groups, who will rally the people in their various neighborhoods.[25]

It is quite obvious that the founding leaders of the CCF, who had contested and won elections, viewed it as more of a missionary crusade, relying a good deal on faith (or "trust", as Woodsworth would have it) in the people of individual neighborhoods ... while the eastern philosophical leaders (like Lewis, Underhill and Frank Scott) considered the CCF as a political instrument badly requiring organization and some central "direction".

Lewis contrasted the CCF's reality with the situation in Europe:

In the countries of Europe that I had visited, the social democratic parties had in place a considerable apparatus designed to provide leadership and support in the work of organization, education, research and the publication of party newspapers, journals and pamphlets.[26]

Lewis set out from the first to rectify the situation, as best he could, using the only models he knew.

In the matter of funding, there was one source that the CCF had never really attempted to tap ... organized labour. For Lewis, fresh from European and British observations, it was natural that trade unions should be the real foundation of any social democratic party. this assumption is, in fact, the most basic tenet of Marxism. Lewis set out to forge political and financial links with organized labour.

He also set out to get an office for the national CCF. This was space donated by Russell of the law firm, initially, and its only recommendation was an imposing address: 124 Wellington Street, across from the Parliament Buildings. The two "rooms" of this national headquarters were partitioned from a lean-to originally used as storage for a restaurant. There was no heating and there was no floor ... just sand. But Lewis (and Sophie) set out to furnish it as an office, and managed to scrounge the necessary furniture and equipment from Ottawa-area CCF supporters. Lewis was later to boast that the only thing they had to pay for was the telephone.

By 1938, when he joined the party full-time on a salaried basis, Lewis was confident that he could raise enough money to operate the office and pay himself his very modest income. Altogether, Lewis was to labour for 12 years as National Secretary, resigning regretfully only in 1950 because he felt he owed his family (by then consisting of four children) some financial foundation. In 1950, at the age of 41, David Lewis turned to a serious concentration on his law career for the first time in his life. The party had consumed all of his time and energy up until 1950, and he had precious little in any material sense to show for it. Even in 1950 Lewis was paid only $3,200 a year as the CCF's National Secretary, seriously inadequate for a family of six. He had given his all to the party for more than a decade.

The main disappointment for Lewis during these years was the failure of the CCF to develop its full potential. As we have seen, Canadians did not march off to World War II with the same naive patriotism with which they'd responded to World War I. They marched, but with some profound misgivings and sharp memories of the Depression and unemployment they'd experienced after the first global conflict. It was natural to ask the question: *Why couldn't the government find the money to alleviate the sufferings of the Depression, when money was so quickly found to fight the Second World War?* To many Canadians, and perhaps mostly to those in the services overseas, the boom-and-bust cycle of capitalism, and its essentially agressive nature which profited by weapons manufacture and warfare, seemed to be plainly apparent. The CCF's explanation of the flaw in the economic structure seemed to make a great deal of sense. But beyond anything else, the CCF's concern was structuring a peace-time world of economic security and economic fairness. It had not escaped the notice of average Canadians that while men were conscripted to fight on the battlefields of Europe, the wealth of the industrialists had not been similarly conscripted. Manufacturers had simply refused to produce the needed war materiel at a pegged low profit. Instead, vast profits were made while average people died.

The CCF's popularity rose sharply between 1942 and 1944. In 1944 its popularity nationally, according to the Gallup Poll, topped the Tories and Liberals by a percentage point. The CCF was the most popular party in Canada and posed a very real threat to the political *status quo.*

A crucial turning point in the future success was the Ontario election of June 4, 1945. It preceded the federal election of June 11, 1945 by just a week.

Quite obviously, if the CCF did well in Canada's largest and most populous province, it could be expected to do well in the federal election just one week later. It would be taken seriously as a party capable of governing. That is how David Lewis read the public's mood, and he was probably correct.

The CCF was already a force to be reckoned with. It formed the government of Saskatchewan as of June 1944. It was the Official Opposition in Ontario, Manitoba and British Columbia. If it could break through in Ontario ... either forming a government or increasing its representation in Opposition, then the federal electorate would be impressed. Even though the Gallup showed CCF popularity slipping from its 1944 high, it was still in a very strong position.

And, it should be said here, that one of the reasons why the CCF popularity had slipped federally was simply that the Liberal government of Mackenzie King in Ottawa had moved with great haste to adopt and implement some of the major CCF social programs that were intended to soften the transition to peace. Family allowances were one such CCF program, which Mackenzie King had quickly grasped, and this became an issue in the Ontario election of June 4, 1945.

The Conservative Premier of Ontario, George Drew, opposed the implementation of family allowances by Ottawa on the grounds that Catholic Quebec would benefit from the program more than Ontario! The CCF Official Opposition at Queen's Park simply had to vote against Drew's stance. The major affront to the CCF was Drew's opposition to a needed national program on the shabby and divisive grounds of racism and appeals to anti-Catholic prejudice. The CCF Opposition voted against Drew's precarious minority government, Drew's government fell, and the election of June 4, 1945 was on.

It was one of the most shameful and vicious elections in Canadian history, and it was the occasion of Canada's own Watergate. Unfortunately, however, Canada then lacked investigative journalists of the calibre of Woodward and Bernstein, and lacked major media with the integrity and courage of *The Washington Post*. In a word, while Nixon was toppled by his Watergate, Drew got away with the same crimes of purjury and illegal surveillance. One wonders how many more Watergates, and worse, there have been in Liberal and Conservative history which remain unknown to the public.

At any rate, the "Watergate" of 1945 concerned the fact that George Drew authorized an illegal surveillance of the CCF by a "special department" of the Ontario Provincial Police.[27] This outfit, with William J. Osborne-Dempster in charge, was to dig up evidence, or invent it if it could not be found, that the CCF was a part of the international communist conspiracy. While it was at it, the "special department" also investigated trade unions and other individuals apparently for the hell of it. In short, the "special department" investigated just about anyone who posed a political threat, or a threat of criticism, to Drew's government.

Some of the "special department's" reports, for instance, concerned the conservative civil libertarian, B.K. Sandwell, then editor of *Saturday Night* and R.C. Wallace, the Principal of Queen's University.

In short, special department was an outift designed to dig up dirt on political opponents, and intimidate them, under a guise of national security. Only in this case the rationale was "provincial security" since it seemed to be purely an Ontario operation. And, similar to Watergate, Osborne-Dempster, the officer in charge of the outfit, seemed to be a Howard Hunt sort of buffoon. He was fond of signing his secret reports as agent "D.208" long after his cover was blown, and his political snooping and analysis was laughable.

D.208's secret reports were passed to the commissioner and deputy commissioner of the Ontario Provincial Police, and then on to the Ontario attorney-general and the premier himself. The premier, in turn, made the reports available Gladstone Murray and M.A. Sanderson for use in anti-CCF advertisements accepted for publication in the major newspapers of eastern Canada. The quality of the data obtained by Osborne-Dempster is apparent from the fact that the CCF won several libel suits generated by these ads.

The "special department" started to unravel when constable Rowe began to have second thoughts about the propriety of what he was involved in. He took some of D.208's reports to Edward Bigelow (Ted) Jolliffe, the leader of Ontario's CCF. Jolliffe moved very cautiously, partly because he just couldn't believe that Drew's government would actually be involved in something so sordid. Jolliffe made discreet enquiries and obtained signed affadavits attesting to the reality of the situation from some of the principals involved. On May 24, 1945 Ted Jolliffe went on the radio and accused Drew...

> Colonel Drew is maintaining in Ontario, at this very minute, a secret political police, a paid government spy organization, a Gestapo to try to keep himself in power.[28]

Jolliffe went on to outline, with complete accuracy, the identity of D.208, the destination of his reports that ended up in newspaper advertisements after passing through Drew's office.

The Ontario public was shocked and "for the remaining ten days, the Ontario campaign dealt with little else than Jolliffe's 'Gestapo' charges, as the affair was universally called".

Drew's response came as a shock to the naive and honest

CCFers. Drew denied any knowledge of the "special department" whatsoever. He stonewalled the whole thing as Nixon was to do 23 years later. Drew went on the counter-attack. After calling Jolliffe a liar, Drew promised to establish a post-election enquiry and to resign his seat if the commission of enquiry should find him guilty of Jolliffe's accusations. Drew's righteous indignation was immense, his denials vehement.

It was a more trusting age. The Ontario electorate was confused, but impressed at Drew's protestations of complete innocence. In the end, they decided that Drew was honourable ... *must* be honourable ... and that, in consequence, the CCF was unfair and dishonourable.

The results of the June 4 election were a disaster for the CCF. The party elected just 8 members in 1945, the Liberals were the big winners in the "Gestapo" affair and elected 11 members to become the Official Opposition. The CCF was rejected in the crucial Ontario contest.

George Drew was as good as his word. After the election, almost immediately after, he established a commission of inquiry under a prominent Liberal jurist, Mr. Justice LeBel of the Supreme Court of Ontario. In due course, LeBel found that Jolliffe had accurately described the entire "special department" operation ... except that LeBel could find no evidence that George Drew had had any personal knowledge of it. Jolliffe's major accusation was, therefore, contradicted by the LeBel Commission. The CCF was discredited.

The reason why LeBel could find no evidence that Drew knew about D.208 and the "special department" was simply that George Drew cheerfully lied under oath to LeBel and spirited evidence away from the LeBel Commission. the facts of the matter did not come to light until 30 years later, when Drew's papers (now in the Public Archives of Canada) were thoroughly researched. The papers contain numerous personal letters between Gladstone Murray, whom Drew swore to LeBel that he had only "contacted" twice in 11 years, and George Drew dated up to the day of Jolliffe's accusations. Some of these letters contained direct reference to D.208 and his reports ... and their use in anti-CCF advertisements, as well as casual references to recent meetings between the two men.

The entire story, like Watergate itself and the uncovering of Nixon's knowledge and purjury, is very complex, but the crux of the matter is that the Premier of Ontario did have knowledge of the "special department", there is some evidence that he encouraged its formation, and that he lied under oath to Mr. Justice LeBel. In short, Jolliffe's accusations have been completely vindicated by history.

But, of course, the damage to the CCF had been done. The naive Ontario electorate believed Drew, voted for him and Liberals rather than for the CCF. It may be noteworthy, too, that although Drew was aware of the "special department" and its attempts to link the CCF to communism, he himself constantly equated the CCF with Hitler's National Socialist (Nazi) party. Whereas this was not only unfair, but a slander, Drew apparently knew that the Ontario electorate would be confused and disturbed. It was, and Drew won with the Liberals elevated to the Official Opposition. The *status quo* had weathered the CCF threat in Ontario.

The status quo weathered the CCF threat in the federal election a week later, too. It is worth noting that one effective tactic was for the Liberals and Conservatives to run just one mutually-approved candidate against the stronger CCF candidates, pooling the Liberal and Conservative vote to try and defeat the socialist menace.

Another tactic was flooding the country with anti-CCF propaganda and advertisements, some of which conveyed purposefully inaccurate and distorted information. This propaganda campaign was backed by major Canadian corporations, especially life insurance companies, and cost much more than CCF campaign expenditures. Life insurance salesmen were instructed to tell policy-holders that their policies would be worthless under a CCF government. Company presidents called workers together and said that their firms would be forced out of business by the CCF and the workers would become unemployed. Some 3,000,000 pamphlets attacking the CCF were, somehow, mailed through the Post Office illegally ... because the pamphlets did not have publisher address and identification as per federal requirements ... but got through the mails anyway.

The CCF did not win the federal election of 1945, nor did the party form the Official Opposition. The *status quo* of Liberal-Conservative co-operation held ... barely. But the CCF did increase its federal representation, although almost all CCF members were elected west of Ontario: 5 from Manitoba, 18 from Saskatchewan, 4 from British Columbia ... a total of 28 members.

David Lewis considered a major breakthrough in Ontario crucial for the party's chances to emerge as a major political force and to take advantage of its poll popularity. The CCF's failure to make a good showing in Ontario in 1945 was, in Lewis's opinion, the start of the CCF's decline that demanded a new political approach altogether. This, eventually, became the New Democratic Party.

Lewis attributed the CCF's defeat in Ontario to the "Gestapo" affair and to the anti-CCF propaganda. Being honourable men themselves, and ones committed to public education rather than manipulation, the leaders of the eastern CCF were appalled at the slander used against them. They were appalled at Drew's lies to the electorate when the CCF had the damning evidence. They were appalled that the so-called "responsible" press in eastern Canada swiftly published the libelous advertisements placed by Gladstone Murray and Sanderson, but did not exhibit sufficient journalistic integrity to assign some good investigative reporters to delve into the truth of Jolliffe's accusations. Further, the men of the eastern CCF were appalled that the major newspapers consistently refused to run CCF advertisements. Lewis's memoirs, written three decades later, convey a vivid sense of his shock and outrage that supposedly civilized and responsible people could have acted as they did in June 1945.

It is clear, however, that the whole story of the CCF's Ontario defeat cannot be attributed to the shabby propaganda and the "Gestapo" affair. After all, Tommy Douglas had romped to victory in Saskatchewan almost exactly a year before the disastrous CCF defeat in Ontario, and Douglas's CCFers had faced exactly the same barrage of propaganda and distortions by the press. What was the difference?

Why could Tommy Douglas, struggling against most of the same adversities, win 47 of 52 seats in a 1944 Saskatchewan CCF landslide while the Ontario CCF lost significant representation a year later?

I think there's an answer for this, though it is a subtle one and one that's very difficult to discuss fairly without over-emphasis, without the danger of some distortion. Perhaps it is best to begin with a factual observation: David Lewis described himself as a "reluctant candidate", he refused to contest elections on several occasions and did not succeed in winning a seat until 1962 . . . 26 years after his political career began.

Lewis was horrified by his first election experience, in Cartier (Montral) in 1943, and was never anxious to repeat it. It seems that although Lewis was genuinely concerned with the welfare and fulfillment of people, he didn't personally trust them. This attitude stemmed from the source of his socialistic commitment — he was motivated by a rather intellectual sort of Marxist dialectic and methodology, not by a deep faith in humanism. the eastern leaders of the CCF who, along with Lewis, masterminded the Ontario debacle in 1945 were cut from the same sort of cloth (as Woodsworth might have said). Underhill, Scott and Lewis were not politicians in the best possible sense of that tainted word . . . they didn't *like* people, didn't trust them. They saw "people" as a sort of Marxist "mass" that could be organized to create a better world for everyone, but not as flesh-and-blood creatures with whom they shared aspirations.

The campaign style of the Ontario CCF in 1945 was an aloof and academic exercise in educating the electorate in what the CCF stood for and what its platform was. It may have command-ed attention and respect, but it generated little human warmth, compassion or humour. When, over the "Gestapo" affair, the electorate was forced to make a decision of faith (since there was no proof, in any legal sense, available to Jolliffe at that time), the electorate opted for the more empathetic candidates, including Drew.

Education of the electorate is fine, but voters do not want to treated like an amorphous mass being led to a better society for their own good. People, individually, need to feel that they matter, and matter to the political parties and candidats that seek their support. The eastern intellectuals of the CCF were never able to communicate any great feeling of rapport with their potential supporters. They were, in fact, a dour and distant collection of people. They must have seemed paternalistic to the voters of Ontario, just as David Lewis often seemed paternalistic and condescending even to people within his own party.

By contrast, Tommy Douglas was a politician ... and in the best sense of the word. He genuinely liked people, and he trusted them even though he had his own electoral disappointments from time to time. His motivating faith was a faith in humanity, not a faith in a dialectic or methodology, and the people obviously and naturally responded to it. He realized early on that the best defence against propaganda and slander was simply to refuse to take it seriously and to demonstrate its absurdity through humour. His recourse to pithy humour assured his public of several things: anyone who could laugh at himself and his enemies could not represent a deadening, collectivist political doctrine; someone with Douglas's sense of humour and objectivity could not be personally unbalanced in any major way that could lead to excesses in political action; he could be trusted as someone not very different from oneself ... maybe just a bit more committed, more honest, more compassionate.

One wonders how Douglas would have handled the "Gestapo" affair. He certainly would not have presented the situation in the too-earnest way that Jolliffe did, would not have dissected every aspect of it in his memoirs the way Lewis did. Being a politician, Douglas might not have brought the matter up at all during the election. He might have concluded that anyone capable of being involved with the "special department" was also quite capable of lying about it ... an obvious conclusion that neither Jolliffe nor Lewis could credit. But then Douglas had had the rear wheel-nuts of his car loosened by so-called civilized political rivals and had fewer illusions, and pretensions, than the eastern leaders of the CCF.

So, it may be that the intangible quality of "trust" between candidates and their potential electorates played a crucial part in the Ontario 1945 election. The voters didn't trust the eastern CCFers, and the CCF leaders didn't trust them. In democratic politics, education is no substitute for trust ... the highest art of the sincere candidate is to combine both. It may be that this intangible quality of "trust" remains at the core of the NDP's contemporary stagnation, a legacy of an outmoded dialectic-economic orientation that, very subtly, creates an impersonal and materialist party image.

The doctrinaire methodology of eastern CCF leaders created yet *another* problem in the 1945 Ontario election, although one that contributed to electoral confusion and, in this way, helped to undermine further the quality of trust.

David Lewis had, as early as 1936, begun to approach organized labour in the hopes of drumming up increased CCF funding and some increased votes. This was the natural direction to be followed according to both Marxist theory and the evolution of European social democratic parties. That's what a "Labour Party" was all about, and Lewis had no doubt that the CCF was a Labour Party along British and European lines. It was the natural assumption of his Swislocz boyhood and Oxford education.

Over the years, Lewis managed to arrange some official labour affiliations for the CCF. And it can be said that this backfired in the Ontario election of 1945.

Very few unions were officially affiliated with the CCF in 1945. Some openly supported the Liberals or Conservatives, and others were controlled at least partly by Communists. By obtaining some official trade union support, the CCF ran afoul of both the Liberals and the Communists as far as the electorate was concerned.

It is a cliché that politics makes strange bedfellows, but surely there was never so much incongruous pillow-talk as in 1945 between the Liberals and the Communists! The CCF threatened both the Liberals and the Communists. For the Liberals, of course, the CCF threatened to "destroy free enterprise" as the propaganda would have it or, more realistically, might get elected before the Liberals could adopt the CCF policies. For the Communists the CCF represented a threat of introducing such progressive social programs that the "revolution" might gain few enthusiasts ... if the CCF won, why fight?

Thus, the CCF represented a threat to both "left" and "right", and maybe it is not too surprising that the Liberals and Communists actively co-operated to get rid of the CCF in the interests of returning to the capitalist vs. communist conflict that everyone knew and loved. As strange as it may seem, therefore, the Liberals and Communists joined forces to run "Liberal-Labour" candidates in several ridings!

In centres like Windsor the communists caused havoc in CCF activity. In the 1945 provincial election three ridings which had been won by the CCF in 1943 were lost because the United Automobile Workers ran candidates as "Liberal-Labour", supported by the LPP (Communist Party) and the Liberal Party. Two of the seats were lost to the Tories; the third was won by Parent, the candidate nominated by the UAW as "Lib.-Lab.". On arrival at the legislature, he promptly joined the Liberal caucus and no more was heard of him.[29]

It is not surprising that the Ontario electorate was a little baffled by all the strategems employed to defeat the CCF on the part of Liberals, Communists and Tories.

But it *is* surprising, in view of the luke-warm reception that CCF overtures enjoyed among organized labour, and in view of the actual labour vote, that Lewis and his eastern CCF colleagues would persist in the firm belief that organized labour must form the foundation of a Canadian social democratic party. David Lewis was a brilliant and dedicated man ... but he had a blind spot. He never was able to see the Canadian reality as it was, but only as he felt it had to be according to the tenets of Marxist dialectics and European experience.

In spite of the 1945 results, with losses in Ontario due partly to labour affiliation and gains in the west due to prairie populism with missionary overtones, Lewis continued to mold the CCF toward an official and national labour affiliation.

* * * * * *

Although David Lewis resigned as full-time National Secretary of the CCF in 1950, he did not cease activity in the party. He continued to fill important positions in the National Executive, and he continued to work for an official labour-CCF coalition or affiliation. Lewis's labour in this direction was finally rewarded in 1958 when the Canadian Labour Congress passed a resolution at its Winnipeg convention in April. The resolution was worded by David Lewis and Eamon Park, and called for a new type of political organization that was ...

a broadly based people's movement, which embrances the CCF, the Labour Movement, farm organizations, professional people and other liberally-minded persons interested in basic social reform and reconstruction through our parliamentary system of government.[30]

The resolution instructed ...

the Executive Council to give urgent and immediate attention to this matter by initiating discussions with the CCF, interested farm organizations and other like-minded individuals and groups, to formulate a constitution and a program for such a political instrument of the Canadian people ...[31]

Originally, the intention of everyone was to move rather slowly. The overture of the Canadian Labour Congress was to have been debated carefully at the CCF's scheduled convention later in the summer of 1958. Diefenbaker's landslide victory of March 31, 1958 speeded things up considerably, accounting for the CLC's resolution in Winnipeg less than a month later. Dief's victory decimated the CCF, reducing the party to just 8 Members in Ottawa ... or, exactly the number it had elected some 22 years before when David Lewis was offered his job by Woodsworth.

After Diefenbaker's landslide, and after all the years with little to show for all the effort, the CCF could not afford the luxury of taking things slowly. If there was a place for a social democratic party in Canada, and if that place could be secured by a coalition with organized labour, then the time to move was at hand. At the CCF convention, a resolution to accept the CLC invitation was passed and a National Committee for a "New Party" was formed. Originally, farm organizations were invited to send representatives to this National Committee, but they declined to participate. The Committee initially consisted of 10 CCF representatives and 10 from the Canadian Labour Congress. However ...

A triumvirate of sponsors was desired, so the party could afford a wider newer look, and the solution agreed on was to organize New Party Clubs of non-CCFers, presumably to take in the "professionals and other liberally-minded" citizens. Ten representatives of these clubs became members of the Committee ...[32]

The original appeal to farm groups turned out to be only lip-service, and the representation by New Party Clubs was a disguise to obscure the fundamental labour affiliation of the new political instrument. David Lewis, at long last, had succeeded in transforming the CCF into a proper social democratic party as he understood the concept ...

> Although I expected it and had had a hand in preparing the (CLC) resolution, I was nevertheless relieved and excited when the Congress vote brought the Canadian labour movement fully into the political arena. Like many other people in the CCF, I felt as if after a long and weary journey we had finally reached our destination.[33]

The result of all this was, of course, the present New Democratic Party. The founding convention was July 31 to August 4, 1961, held in Ottawa and largely paid for by the CLC. However ...

> Privately, a score or so of trade union leaders liked to claim a parental role in the New Party; however, their public stance was to disclaim responsibility. They were so convinced that a "labour party" as such would be unacceptable to voters that they were almost neurotic in attempting to downplay their presence, and in setting up a constitutional form that would put control of the party in the hands of constituency members — exactly as the CCF had always been organized — with only a supportive, affiliate role reserved for the unions ... In fact, the constitutional instructures of the new party and the CCF hardly varied at all.
> A casual observer ... might be excused for asking why the exercise ever took place. The CLC worked very hard, and contributed funds, to launch the New Party with a spectacular mammoth founding convention at which the rafters rang and the people sang ... (and) tactfully and modestly withdrew.[34]

Why, indeed, did the exercise take place if union leaders themselves were convinced that Canadians would never support a "labour party as such"?

What was that wonderful "destination" that David Lewis ("like many others in the CCF") felt he had reached after a long and weary journey?

The only tangible advantage was the change of name. The old name, "Co-operative Commonwealth Federation" had proved impossible to translate into French. The "New Democratic Party" was much better in this regard, becoming "Nouveau Parti Democratique" ... but since neither the CCF nor the NDP ever enjoyed much success in Quebec, this was hardly a major gain.

The real reason for the change from CCF to labour-affiliated NDP was David Lewis's fixation, the hard work that made this fixation a reality, and the misconceptions that made this fixation a fallacy. The case was put clearly by Doris French Shackleton:

> ... If farmer support could not sustain a national party, the obvious course was to shift the base to labour. This had always been the goal of the eastern party leaders. How else were the great provinces of central Canada to be won? How else had democratic socialist parties come to power in other countries? The trade union base was the international tradition.
>
> The flaw in the argument was that next door to Canada was the biggest industrial nation in the world, where trade unions did *not* support a democratic socialist party, but allied themselves with "free enterprise" parties similar in their economic outlook to Canada's Liberals and Conservatives. Canada's trade unions were largely affiliated with those American unions. There was a thread of political action sentiment running through Canadian trade union history, and a group of top union leaders were active members of the CCF and cherished the notion of a union-supported party. But other union leaders, and vast throngs of union members, did not.[35]

In effect then, David Lewis's magnificently Marxist obsession saddled the NDP with a union affiliation which even union leaders sought to downplay to the Canadian public. He managed to arrange an affiliation with organizations whose membership did not even deliver a majority of their vote to the NDP. It was a triumph of misguided and misapplied methodology, and a tragedy of *realpolitik*.

It was also an achievement replete with some irony. Who was to lead the New Democratic Party? There can be little doubt, in spite of his disclaimers, that David Lewis longed to lead it. That would have been only human since the NDP was largely the child of 25 years of his own labour.

But David Lewis had never won an election. He could not be chosen leader of a new political party going into electoral battle for the first time. But within the NDP there was only one consistent winner ... the old prairie Christian, Tommy Douglas ...

> ... why was Douglas the man they chose as leader? He was surely, among prominent CCFers, the one most identified with moralistic socialism. His association with trade unions had been subject to some strain during the years of his Premiership ...
> Yet he was the first and only choice of the trade union architects of the new party. Quite simply, he was a success, where others had a record of failure.[36]

The tale of the CCF had come full circle with ironic repercussions. The eastern methodologist who had been employed to assist a western-based caucus now saw his doctrinaire creation recruiting the western moralist as a leader. It would be easy to say that nothing had really changed, and that the NDP was just the CCF by another name, but that would be to miss a subtle transformation. Even though it was forced to recruit the successful prairie moralist, the philosophy of the party had changed. Its ideological centre of gravity had shifted from "Methodism" to "Marxism", from moralism to methodology. The control, the image, the funding and ther philosophical outlook of the NDP were dominated by the east.

There is no doubt that there was a significant amount of fundamental disagreement, and perhaps even personal animosity, between Tommy Douglas and David Lewis. In one of his first acts as *de facto* National Secretary, Lewis sent a memo to all CCF Members of Parliament and national executives confirming Garland as the national organizer. Lewis's memo curtly demanded that each recipient initial his approval as quickly as possible ... to which Tommy Douglas scribbled an "Aye, aye, Sir!" at the bottom of the memo. Later, after Douglas had been elected Premier of Saskatchewan, Lewis saw nothing amiss about sending Douglas some fatherly advice about how to run his government ...

... which brings me to a long, eight-page letter which I wrote to the premier some six months after he took office ... I found a great deal that worried me and I set it all out in detail, with the usual plea to Douglas "not to be annoyed with my presumption in voicing criticisms and suggestions".

My major stricture was that the government had no over-all plan and no machinery for arriving at one. I found that Britnell, a traditional economist, had little faith in government planning and confined his committee's functions to dealing with specific problems referred to it. My letter was also critical of the way the Department of Natural Resources, under Joe Phelps as minister, had acquired small manufacturing plants whose viability was doubtful. I wrote that this had "grave and serious dangers", and added, All that is needed is one single failure in one of the under-takings, and all the good that the government has already done and will do may easily be swept aside in the public mind.[37]

There's no reason to doubt that Lewis was motivated by genuine concern and a desire to be of service to the fledgling government of Saskatchewan ... but to lecture Douglas on the "public mind". Here was a man who shrank from elections preaching to a man who had won a landslide victory against great odds!

The tension between Lewis and Douglas was sometimes palpable, especially toward the end of Douglas's leadership when it was patently obvious that Lewis expected to be his heir. The tension split the party into Douglas and Lewis camps.

Few contradictions have matched, in Canadian public life, this contrast between Tommy Douglas and David Lewis, each in his way so close to the heart and nerve centre of his party. The freely recorded comments of party follow-ers show the sharp cleavage, for to consider Douglas unique in leadership was to see a great fault in Lewis, and the opposite stance was equally true.[38]

If Lewis was uncomfortable with the Douglas style of political presentation, Douglas was no less uncomfortable with the big new style of the party he led. Characteristically, however, Douglas expressed his discomfort mildly and with humour. At one of the first "new-style" NDP fund-raising affairs, a $50-a-plate dinner in Toronto, Douglas began his obligatory speech with: "It's always a pleasure to speak to a group of the under-privileged proletariat."

On another occasion, again in Toronto, party organizers and publicity men were brain-storming about how to get attention and give the NDP a "with-it image". It was the 1960s and Toronto had opened up, with Yonge Street featuring strippers and topless go-go. One of the publicity types, only half in jest, suggested that an NDP rally should be led by a naked lady riding a horse down Yonge Street. Douglas considered this proposal carefully and finally said: "I think that would be a very good idea, it must have been years since the people of Toronto have seen a horse."

In spite of the supposed new look, and in spite of supposedly official trade union support, it was Tommy Douglas who led the party to winning 19 seats in its first federal election in 1962. This was 11 more than the CCF had taken in its last (1958) election, but post-mortem analysis revealed ...

> The NDP had increased their seats to nineteen from the eight held by the CCF in the last caucus. The labour vote, instead of going to "their" new party had, according to a post-election Gallup Poll, gone predominantly to the Liberals, who got 38 per cent of the votes from trade union homes, while Conservatives got 25 per cent and the NDP only 23 per cent.[39]

In short, the new look and the new supposed trade union affiliation had not changed the voting patterns. Diefenbaker's victory of 1958, which had decimated all political opponents, had not ended of the CCF's natural support as had been feared. The election of 1962 reduced Diefenbaker's huge 1958 majority to a minority government (PCs 116, Liberals 100, Social Credit 30 and NDP 19). The CCF support re-emerged in about the same ball-park as it had always been since the party's actual establishment as a political force in the late 1930s — somewhere between 20 and 30 seats. The trade union affiliation had made no difference whatsoever in terms of actual electoral success.

One noteworthy event did occur in the 1962 federal election. David Lewis managed to win in York South, his first campaign

victory in his political career, and he was promptly named
Deputy Leader of the New Democratic Party. Having won,
Lewis became an increasingly viable alternative to Tommy
Douglas during the 1960s.

In spite of official trade union support, the NDP was ill-
equipped financially to contest the many elections of the 1960s as
the country see-sawed between Pearson and Diefenbaker (1962,
1963, 1965) and finally broke the Mexican stand-off with an
overwhelming display of Trudeaumania (1968). But more
important than funding limitations, the successive election
results showed that the trade union support simply never
materialized significantly while official union affiliation might
have scared other voters away. The NDP's Parliamentary representation remained at old CCF levels: 19 seats in the 1962
election, 17 seats in 1963, 21 seats in 1965, and 22 seats in 1968.

The early 1960s had been molded by the Kennedy-style
political image, and the later 1960s were molded by his memory.
The era of the young politician was in vogue ... or, at least, the
young-*looking* politician. Tommy Douglas was increasingly
regarded as an old-fashioned anachronism and a liability to the
prospects for NDP growth. There was a considerable number of
people within the NDP who favoured a leadership change, and
there is evidence that Douglas favoured such a change himself.
He wanted a younger man at the head of the party, perhaps someone more "radical" (even if that meant a Marxist-leaning
"radical") and energetic. Douglas had always felt that a social
democratic party should have a truly noisy and pushy "left"
composed of young people ...

> The Waffle was a recent development, late in my term as
> leader. It was the sort of thing we've always had in the CCF
> and NDP, as in all democratic socialist and labour parties
> — a left wing.
> I've never quarreled with their right to be a bit ahead of
> the party. My dread has never been that the party will be too
> radical. My dread has been that the party will settle into a
> rut and become complacent. People who act as gadflies are
> useful in keeping you from becoming so over-cautious in
> order to get the support of the middle class that you dilute
> the party, tone it down until it becomes indistinguishable
> from, say, a Liberal Party. ... I've never denied their right to

be, never taken any move to discriminate against them ...
(but) they tend to become idealistic and unrealistic ... they
tend to become people who feel that being doctrinaire and
extreme makes them very special people.

I felt that Saskatchewan worked its way out of the Waffle
situation more easily than Ontario did. I remember the long
sessions in Saskatchewan at conventions and councils when
they wanted to expel somebody. I've always opposed
expelling anybody ...

Some members in some areas suffer from expulsionitis.
And sometimes you expel somebody who, if you'd had a
little more patience, would have stayed and come to his
senses as he got older.

My answer to these so-called left-wingers, and some of
them are not as radical as I am — I suggest one night a week
out canvassing to find out what the average person is
thinking. We are supposed to deal with the problems people
have, not the problems we think they have.[40]

At that time, the late 1960s, the Waffle was most prominently
represented by James Laxer and Mel Watkins who considered
themselves "radicals", and who wanted the NDP to adopt more
doctrinaire policies of nationalization. There is not much doubt
that Douglas was saying only the truth when he hinted that he
was more radical than people like Laxer and Watkins. But
because they tended to *define* radicalism and progressiveness as
Marxist perrogatives, it is possible that they could not credit this
about Douglas. He was radical because he was a moralist, and *his*
vision of Jerusalem might have involved a greater degree of
communal co-operation than even Laxer and Watkins would
have thought either wise or tolerable.

But Douglas, older and wiser than Laxer and Watkins at the
time, had learned that in a democracy one cannot impose too-
radical personal visions on the electorate. As Tommy Douglas
once said:

You have to carry other people with you, in politics. My
father used to say, 'Go as far and as fast as you can, but
never get too far ahead of your own troops.'[41]

We will never know about Douglas's own private visions of
Jerusalem on earth as he conceived it, but there is a fair bit of

evidence to suggest that Douglas wanted a younger man to succeed him as NDP leader, or at least to contest the leadership ... and that the young man he liked was James Laxer. Douglas's prediction was accurate. The James Laxer of the 1960 Waffle days did come to a much greater appreciation of what the Canadian people could accept, and the rate at which they could change. Almost two decades after the Waffle confrontation within the NDP, Laxer was to produce an economic analysis which pinpointed the NDP's electoral problems. Laxer's report provides a key to unlock the mystery of NDP stagnation. It only remains to be seen whether the NDP as a party, and perhaps Laxer as an individual is sufficiently radical to pick it up and open the door of political relevance ... but the party and the leader will have to be as radical as Tommy Douglas.

By 1968 there was much thought of leadership change within the NDP, and Eastern party advisors were pushing the cause of David Lewis. Frank Scott, Lewis's old professor from McGill days, articulated the mood of the "progressive" wing of the party:

> To some degree perhaps Tommy is too much the popular preacher. He needs a style that is more serious. It must have been galling for David — that slightly offhand manner of Tommy's was a little galling to sit under. We should have had David earlier.[42]

A similar sentiment was expressed by Margaret Stewart, once secretary of the Ontario NDP:

> I always felt it was a mistake that David didn't take the leadership at the beginning (in 1961). David has tremendous intellectual stature. A magnificent voice. I think he's superb. The press was hard on Tommy, but some of it was justified. He was an old-fashioned Saskatchewan socialist.[43]

The groundswell for Lewis within the eastern and controlling wing of the party became so strong that a curious incident occured during the 1968 federal election campaign. It was the first emergence of Trudeaumania, and the idea that the NDP needed a younger, more progressive leader was promoted by party pundits in the east. While Tommy Douglas was campaigning out in British Columbia, David's son, Stephen, flew out to the coast. His mission: *to ask Douglas to resign as leader and name Lewis in his place.*

It is impossible to know whether Stephen was sent on this mission by his father, or whether it was a spontaneous and independent act on Stephen's part. Whatever, Douglas coldly refused the "request" from the son of the party's heir apparent. And he did it for at least two good reasons. First, it was not in the tradition of either the CCF or the NDP to *transfer* the leadership and short-circuit the democratic process of electing a leader. And second, a fact that everyone but Douglas seemed to have forgotten, was that Lewis was just four years younger than Douglas! If Douglas was to be replaced by a younger man, then it made sense for the successor to be significantly younger. Douglas and Lewis were definitely of the same generation.

An objective observer cannot help but suspect that, perhaps, David Lewis *sent* Stephen to attempt to wrest the NDP leadership from Douglas. Lewis was never good at elections, and it is possible that he wanted to avoid a contested leadership. If he had such fears, they were well-founded. At the leadership convention of April 1971, Lewis needed four ballots to defeat the young Waffle upstart, Jim Laxer. It showed a remarkable inability on the part of David Lewis to command loyalty and votes even within his own party.

There is a hint that Douglas may have done all he could to help Laxer during the 1971 convention. In his speech just before the balloting began, Douglas recommended some books on the subject of resources and energy policy. One of these books was *The Continental Energy Poker Game* by James Laxer. As an NDP worker, Hans Brown, remembered it . . .

> Everybody whipped out their pencils, looked for a clean corner of a page to write down the books Tommy thought they should read. A moment or two later here's Jim Laxer's name on the ballot![44]

And Tommy Douglas's biographer assures us:

> Douglas persisted in believing that the Waffle leaders should and could be absorbed into the party. Immediately

after the 1971 leadership convention at which Laxer had made a strong showing, the federal council rejected Waffle nominees to the executive of the party. Douglas wrote to a Nova Scotian party member: "Like yourself, I was very disappointed that Jim Laxer and Mel Watkins were not elected to the Federal Executive."

Later Douglas told Hans Brown that he hoped Laxer would pick a seat in a good riding in the 1972 federal election and win a seat in parliament — instead Laxer withdrew his candidature and his party membership.[45]

In retrospect, and given some knowledge of Douglas and his values, it seems obvious that he refused to hand the leadership to Lewis on a platter, as Stephen Lewis had requested, because it contravened Douglas's democratic commitment. David Lewis would have to fight for the leadership in an open convention . . . like anyone else. The leadership was not a "reward" for Lewis's years of work. And more, although it seems obvious from his statements made at the time that Douglas considered Laxer a bit too immature to be party leader, he nonetheless thought that Laxer would prove to be a future NDP asset. Douglas was a shrewd politician and his book-naming speech just before leadership balloting may have been a ploy, not to defeat Lewis, but to make him fight for the plum . . . and to encourage Laxer to hang in.

If this was Douglas's intention, he reckoned without the personality of David Lewis. The Waffle was "purged" from the NDP federally, and in Ontario, along the lines of Lewis's long-standing lack of tolerance for "splinter groups". Aside from maintaining "ideological purity", purging the Waffle from the party conveniently removed any threat to the NDP's controlling clique which was, in turn, controlled by Lewis and the organizational infrastructure he had built up over more than 30 years.

Initially, the Lewis leadership victory and the purging of the Waffle appeared to have enhanced the NDP's electoral image. The election of October 30, 1972 saw an NDP gain of 9 seats, up from 22 to 31 new Members. But it was a short-lived gain. In the election less than two years later (July 8, 1974) the NDP strength was cut in half, down to 16 seats, its lowest point in its history. Lewis was through. His old failing, that inability to generate votes, ended his political career. In the convention of July 1975, the New Democratic Party chose Ed Broadbent as its new leader.

Broadbent, a personable and extremely able man with an engaging presentation and (when appropriate) a lively sense of humour, is nonetheless a trade union oriented socialist politician in the style of David Lewis. He, too, is an easterner, representing the automobile capital of Canada in Oshawa, Ontario. The present New Democratic Party has settled into the mold envisioned by David Lewis ... and it has also settled into an electoral rut. The party has never won more than 32 seats (1980) and now holds 30 as a result of September 4, 1984.

* * * * * *

As a young man in the early 1960s I was politically active, but it cannot be said that I was politically serious or knowledgeable. I was attracted to an extremely radical group, but my interest was more biological than ideological. I was captivated by the ample charms of the group's leader, the blonde daughter of a Rosedale professor of Swedish extraction. In order to demonstrate my solidarity with the peoples' struggle this young woman's group represented, I volunteered to drive the "cadre" to as many demonstrations as possible ... the American consulate was the favourite target, and not least because it was a pleasant walk from Yorkville coffee-houses where the results of our rebellion could be comfortably discussed afterward. Since this revolutionary group numbered about seven, if I recall correctly, it was impossible to fit us all into my battered "sports" car, and so it was necessary to borrow my father's Lincoln Continental for the cadre's periodic sallies against the system.

We attracted some attention, and I'm sure that there are some boring 1960s-type photos on file somewhere at CIA or RCMP headquarters ... and we attracted attention from the Communist Party and from the Trotskyites, but I had better make it clear that, at that time, I had not the foggiest notion of the difference between Communists and Trotskyites (and am not much the wiser now). Since I wanted to be a writer, I was flattered to be asked to contribute pieces to the *Daily Worker*. The journalistic relationship did not prove to be as harmonious as it might have been. Not being serious, I found the Communist jargon and literary style pretty amusing, but, for all that, easy to copy. The *Daily Worker* was apparently offended, however, when I described a European riot with the sentence ...

The bourgeois capitalist fascist police attacked the soles of our comrades' boots with their faces.

I wasn't asked to contribute again and, besides, the blonde revolutionary had decided to enter an M.B.A. course at the University of Toronto. Listless, I gravitated to the NDP.

Admittedly, the NDP was initially a lot duller than plotting revolution with a dedicated cadre in the shelter of a parked Lincoln, but gradually, some slight knowledge of politics and political parties began to sink in. I must have done something right because I was elected President of Toronto-area NDP Youth at one stage and later, in 1964, became President of the NDP on campus at Dalhousie University in Halifax.

During the course of these NDP-related activities of the early 1960s, I came into casual contact with Tommy Douglas and David Lewis on a number of occasions. At the time, I had only personal impressions to go on since my knowledge of CCF and NDP history was practically nill. Within my Toronto/Ontario NDP milieu, I gathered only that David Lewis was some sort of god with a subtle power that made him greater than the leader of the party.

My personal impressions of Tommy Douglas and David Lewis were of two very different sorts of men, and subsequent political research that has rubbed off over the subsequent two decades has only served to confirm these first impressions. Tommy was always completely *there* as a person, but there was always something witheld or even anxious about David Lewis. I got the distinct impression that while David Lewis took himself very seriously, Tommy Douglas didn't take David Lewis very seriously at all ... and didn't take himself too seriously either. Tommy rarely stood on any sort of ceremony or dignity, he was just confident and secure as Tommy Douglas going about his business. Lewis was always, conscious about his image and dignity. He could be a stickler for what can only be called protocol. He was not informal.

Nowadays, perhaps especially in sophisticated urban environments, it is fashionable to look for the "inner man" behind the public facade. I have been much amused by some journalistic judgements of Douglas by those who sought to penetrate the supposed facade. Walter Stewart of the *Star Weekly* wrote:

> Douglas is a curious combination of the austere and the amiable. He's cool, resilient, shrewd; he has no friends outside politics and few within. He has erected such a barrier between himself and the world that no one I talked to — and I have talked to dozens of the people who knew him best — has been able to penetrate it.[46]

Maybe. And, of course, Stewart is entitled to his opinion . . . but I don't share it. I'm inclined to think that Stewart couldn't see the woods for the trees. Tommy Douglas had no facade . . . what you saw was the man. The "essence" of Tommy Douglas was always right up front . . . which is why, for instance, thousands of people in Saskatchewan and elsewhere in Canada felt perfectly free to refer to him as "Tommy" when meeting him, and not "Mr. Douglas". That's why literally hundreds of people in 1944 Saskatchewan felt free to write to "Dear Tommy" and give their friendly advice about how to run the new government they felt they shared with him.

Of the two, it was David Lewis who erected a barrier between himself and the outside world. Perhaps he could fool some journalists on the order of Stewart by unbending a little so that some of the private man showed . . . and such an observer might conclude that he'd seen the "essence" of the whole personality. In my view, this can be the only explanation for those who saw David Lewis as personable, open, accessible — and, in a word, all the things they'd decided Douglas was not. But it was eastern academics and eastern media pundits who viewed David Lewis in this favourable way, not average men and women who voted.

Since I drifted away from the party in 1965 while following its fortunes and evolution from a distance, as it were, I have given a great deal of thought to the personality of the man who molded the modern NDP. It is a bit of parlour psychiatry but I've concluded to my own satisfaction that David Lewis was himself a curious combination of ambition and insecurity. In some very real way he lacked a strong identity and this produced hints of a "void" that disturbed voters, and because of this, they could not trust him with a political mandate.

It is tempting, and maybe even accurate, to attribute this lack of identity to the cultural and religious conflicts of the Swislocz of his boyhood. He was close to his grandfather, who was a devout Jew, and revered his father ... who had repudiated Judaism completely. What, then, was David to be? This conflict may have been exacerbated by the social atmosphere of anti-Semitism that kept shtetl country in hysteria even though Swislocz itself didn't suffer a pogrom in David's youth. The family and community schism between Zionism and socialism must have added to the uncertainty. All this might have had a greater disruptive effect when David was suddenly yanked from familiar Swislocz and landed in a large foreign city, in a completely different continent and culture, without being able to speak a word of the language. The early school experiences must have further battered an already shaky sense of self-esteem.

But David Lewis was a fighter, and an individual with formidable intellectual resources. He fought back, as we have seen, using all of them. But, the heart of this intelligent and sensitive personality may have badly damaged in the struggle. It remained timid, and sought security and order on the deepest level ... while becoming outwardly assertive. Aside from Sophie, who gave a sense of self and place to David, I believe that he grasped at other things which could impart a sense of security that was never really a part of the personality. The order, organization and ideology of Marxism was one thing that might have made sense to this personality and might have offered it stability. The tradition and organization of the British Labour Party was another brick in constructing a stable home for the confused identity.

Together, the methodology of Marxism and the organization and tradition of the British Labour Party conferred a sense of mission, an opportunity for the intellect and the ambition to fulfill themselves.

But it seems clear that the need for protecting the battered identity eclipsed both the ambition and the intellect within David Lewis's psyche. The quickest and most valid route to political success is, of course, contesting elections. Yet, with all of his gifts of intelligence and oratory, Lewis could seldom bring himself to risk failure and rejection ... the politician's basic occupational hazard. Instead, he decided to try to achieve political success through organizational leadership. Perhaps he came to believe, in the end, that the leadership of the NDP was his due because of his years of labour for the party. Perhaps he came to believe that Tommy Douglas owed him a "laying on of hands" and a transfer of the leadership that circumvented an election.

Everyone brings their personal frailities into their jobs and social interactions and, to some degree, the intellectual and spiritual qualities of everyone are compromised by the batterings of that "self" that conducts the life-long personality defence of the identity. David Lewis brought great intellectual and spiritual gifts to the NDP ... but they were distorted by the bruised identity within the man, which prevented him from perceiving that maybe he did not have to become a politician. Freed from this self-imposed expectation, David's brilliance, compassion and ability to communicate could have developed along different lines. He might well have become the most influential socialist philosopher of his era. His socialist credo is one of the most moving humanist pledges that has ever been written.

> The equality of man is the socialist watchword; the moral struggle against injustice and inequality is the socialist's duty; to be a strong and powerful voice for the common man against the abuse and oppression of the privileged minority is the socialist's function; and to forge an ever finer and higher standard of values and a richer pattern of life and behaviour is the socialist's dream.[17]

Obviously, there were many more similarities than differences between Tommy Douglas and David Lewis, which is why they both laboured in the same party for so many difficult years.

In this socialist credo by David Lewis there is no hint of a rigid ideology, no mention of Marxist methodology, no need for philosophical authoritarianism. It is a message from a sensitive and compassionate soul that spoke directly with Canadians all too rarely, and we are all the poorer for it.

* * * * * *

In addition to the evolution of the CCF into a New Democratic Party based theoretically upon official trade union affiliation, the party underwent another transformation between the 1930s and today.

This deserves some brief discussion because it will become a crucial factor in any assessment of the NDP's future as a political instrument.

The Regina Manifesto was a rousing socialist document full of the language and sentiments of the 1930's. Strictly interpreted, as the CCF's critics and opponents habitually chose to do, it left little room for any sort of economic free enterprise. The emphasis was upon nationalization as the only means of preventing the inherent inhumanities of "free enterprise" and of preventing the boom-and-bust cycle of capitalist economics.

By about 1950, however, socialism had begun to evolve away from the idea that nationalization could be a cure-all. Although not even the writers of the Regina Manifesto had ever really considered nationalizing *everything*, after two decades of social development and considerable thought it began to be apparent that it might not be necessary or even desirable to nationalize most businesses. If an acceptable number of social programs could alleviate the worst excesses of rampant and irresponsible "free enterprise", then there was a definite place for a private sector in the economy. *True competition* in business began to look attractive to progressive socialists because it kept prices lower and stimulated employment. Where nationalization still seemed necessary and desirable was in areas involving basic resources and industry that should be controlled by the people of the country, and in areas where "free enterprise" had become actual monopolies consisting of just a few companies surviving the competition.

The CCF and NDP came around to accept the idea of a mixed economy consisting of some socialized and nationalized economic sectors and some private sectors.

As far as the boom-and-bust cycle of capitalism was concerned, an economic tool called Keynesian theory appeared to offer a way by which the government could control the economy without actually owning it. This new economic theory fitted the model of the mixed economy very well. The idea of Keynesian theory was that the government's fiscal policies could regulate the economy. A faltering economy could be stimulated by infusions of government spending so that a recession or Depression could be averted. Or, on the other hand, an over-heated economy could be slowed down by increased taxation. the theory stated that the money spent during periods when government infusions were necessary could be regained through taxation during periods when the economy was in a too-expansive phase.

In short, the up-and-down cycles of expansion and depression which had, quite obviously, plagued capitalist and free-enterprise economic systems since the time anyone analysed them, could be smoothed out by fiscal intervention on the part of government.

The idea of the mixed economy, and the tool of Keynesian economic theory, together formed the cornerstones of what has been called "The Great Compromise" which characterizes all the economies and societies of the developed and non-communist world. This great compromise is acceptance of the idea of free-enterprise coupled with some form of government influence over the operation of the economy as a whole. It cannot be said often enough that all economies of the industrialized Western world have accepted this compromise *in one form or another*, no matter what the national rhetoric might want citizens to believe. The United States, for instance, does not represent anything like a nearly "pure free enterprise" economy as its business community fondly imagines, nor does the business community want the U.S. economy to be free of government stimulus. The fact of the matter is that the American economy is influenced more by government fiscal policy than many so-called "socialist" economies, and to the immense delight of business. It is only that the means of government infusion has been disguised to protect the myth of free-enterprise. In the United States, Keynesian economics is alive and well and living under the alias of military expenditures.

All industrialized nations, and not just Canada, were anxious to avoid a post-war economic slump like the one experienced after World War I. To one degree or another, they all adopted the Keynesian economics as best they could. The Great Compromise of the mixed economy and acceptance of fiscal interference was the foundation for the "economic miracle" that took place after World War II.

There was no Depression immediately after World War II. The 1950s and 1960s were boom years for the North American economy especially. Production was always increasing, unemployment was within tolerable levels and inflation was controlled ... and social programs alleviated at least some of the worst suffering of unemployment, sickness, poverty and educational needs.

The Great Compromise worked, bringing years of unparalleled prosperity and relative economic stability. Canada's New Democratic Party accepted the idea of a mixed economy and the theories of Keynesian economic influence, and the NDP still does.

The only problem is that The Great Compromise stopped working in Canada about 15 years ago. Since the early 1970s the value of the Canadian dollar has fallen steadily, unemployment and inflation have both increased steadily and economic growth has slowed in spite of the Keynesian prescriptions.

What has gone wrong?

The foundations of The Great Compromise have been undermined by changes in the world's economy. After taking a look at the developments that have destroyed The Great Compromise we will understand why the election of Brian Mulroney on September 4, 1984 confronts all Canadians with a "crisis of clarity."

And after looking at those changes which have destroyed The Great Compromise it will be easier to understand how Mulroney's victory presents the New Democratic Party with the most dramatic opportunity, and most soul-tearing challenge, in its history as a political party.

Chapter Five

James Laxer:

Economics of Obsolescence,

Politics of Decline

In Canada the profile of The Great Compromise was sketched by the Liberal Party during the final days of World War II when it was not only apparent that the Allies would be victorious, but equally clear that the CCF had gained significant political relevance.

The Liberals under Mackenzie King quickly began to draw plans for The Great Compromise. They were guided by two political concerns: how to delay "socialism" in the form of a CCF election victory as long as possible, and provide the Canadian people with an expanding post-war economy in order to satisfy their expectations and provide full employment.

The first concern was easy to solve for the simple reason that the CCF had a number of social programs carefully worked out that could simply be stolen ... and then implemented just rapidly enough to keep the electorate from rebelling against the Grits. One such program was the Family Allowance which, as we have learned, became an issue in the 1945 Ontario provincial election and which *caused* that election because of the Drew minority government's opposition to the family allowance program adopted by the Ottawa Liberals. Other such programs, adopted over the years by mostly Liberal governments, have included medicare, Canada pension plan, unemployment insurance, increased welfare schedules, assistance to the arts (Canada Council), a nationalized energy corporation (Petrocan) and a bureaucracy to assess and limit foreign investment (FIRA). In short, just about all the social programs in place presently to soften the inequities of the "free enterprise" system were stolen by the Liberals from the CCF in self-defence.

So much for one aspect of The Great Compromise ... what about the other major component of it? How was the Liberal government to produce, like magic, an expanding post-war Canadian economy that would satisfy the country's employment and material expectations?

Canada had never had such an economy, at least not on any basis which satisfied the entire country. The nation's economy from Confederation up to the First World War had satisfied only Central Canada and was founded firmly upon the principle of exploiting the other regions as colonies ... and after World War I had come to unemployment and the Depression and the unrest until World War II fortuitously stimulated the economy. The Liberals had no illusions that Canada as a whole was willing to return to the comfortable pre-World Wars sort of pie-slicing.

However, when it came to creating an expanding post-war economy, the Liberal Party would not steal policies from the CCF because the socialists' prescriptions would have undermined the foundation of the Liberal Party, and many individual Liberals.

The socialist prescription was to create a viable and expanding economy by public ownership of much industry, especially in the resource and energy sectors, and by government investment to supply the capital needed. In Canada, this policy did not only derive from socialist doctrine concerning "nationalization". It seemed necessary because the so-called private sector "free enterprisers" in Central Canada had never demonstrated much enthusiasm for investing in Canadian industrial development except in Central Canada itself.

When Tommy Douglas and the CCF came to power in Saskatchewan, the "socialist" government there fended off many internal and doctrinaire pleas for "nationalization" and gamely attempted to generate capital investment in the province's industrial development among traditional money-markets. Saskatchewan even attempted to structure a partnership investment with Ottawa concerning some vital resource industry development. but in line with the traditional Central Canadian values, no one was interested in long-term profits to be derived from actually *developing* Saskatchewan. The only interest was the prospect of short-term profits to be derived from raping Saskatchewan.

A very brief digression may be in order here for the purpose of clearing up a misconception purposefully created by anti-CCF propaganda. When Douglas and the CCF could find few takers among traditional capital investors to finance the industrial development of Saskatchewan, the CCF government was forced to choose the route of public/government ownership or "nationalization". It is generally conceded that the nationalization of utilities (Power Corporation) and some resource industries was a "fiscally sound" move and mostly because other provinces were forced to follow suit with public investment in the energy resource sector. However, much criticism has been levelled against the CCF's "hare-brained" attempts to operate manufacturing facilties. As we have seen, even David Lewis was dubious about the viability of some of these schemes. The fact of the matter is that some of them did fail and did not prove viable. These failures, naturally, were played up by "free enterprise" critics.

But the fact is that although some of these ventures were financial disasters, *the majority of them were not.* The successes of Saskatchewan's hare-brained schemes were not given much press coverage ... for obvious reasons. But the "bottom line" is quite revealing. When the CCF government took over in Saskatchewan the province's *non-agricultural* production was $277 million per annum, but by 1960 this had increased to $948 million. Non-agricultural production represented only 25% of Saskatchewan's gross production value in 1944, but represented 62% of the province's gross production value in 1960. According to the federal Department of Trade and Commerce, Saskatchewan showed the highest rate of growth *for private plus public investment per capita of any province* between 1948 and 1960. The Saskatchewan increase was 140 per cent, almost double British Columbia's investment growth during the same period (74% increase). These figures are not creative accounting, but reflected actual growth and development in real dollar terms. When the CCF came to power Saskatchewan was $178 million in debt, the highest per-capita debt in Canada. By 1960 Saskatchewan's debt was down to $18 million and was paid off completely in 1961 (under a Liberal government which had just been elected) from the CCF's sinking fund established years before. The CCF did it by "setting aside ten per cent of the annual budget to retire debts as they came due". Saskatchewan remained debt-free until the mid-1970s when, like every other provincial government and the federal government as well, huge deficit budgets became necessary ... which brings us back to the mainstream of this chapter.

Quite obviously, the Liberals in Ottawa at the end of World War II did not want to follow the socialist prescriptions for obtaining necessary capital investment in the nation's economy. These solutions would be to admit the moral bankruptcy of the "free enterprise" system as it had always been practised in the past.

Another solution had to be found, and it was. The Liberal answer was to attract American investment into Canada. Americans were invited to set up branch manufacturing plants, or to invest in existing Canadian manufacturing plants, and to invest in Canadian energy and resource industries.

The Liberals, then, constructed Canada's Great Compromise on two pillars: CCF social programs and American money.

American investment in the Canadian economy has become an accepted fact of life ... but few Canadians are really aware of the size of that investment. By 1960, American investments in Canadian industry totalled $11.2 billion, or more than half of all U.S. investments in developed countries. U.S. investment in Canada was greater than American investment in all of Latin America.

But this system seemed to work. In 1950 Canada's GNP (in contstant 1961 dollars) was $24.5 billion. By 1960 the country's GNP had grown by 36 per cent to $38.6 billion. Canadians were prosperous, the country was booming. These were the good times. The U.S. was Canada's largest trading partner, which seemed natural, and everyone was happy.

The Liberal solution of attracting American investment also seemed a natural evolution from World War II co-operation between the two countries in co-ordinating the industrial war effort.

There was, however, a hidden snag in this entire structure. And it is this snag that is at the roots of Canada's present economic situation. Canada's "growth" during these boom years was something like The Emperor's New Clothes ... it didn't really exist in the sense of being a real economy. Canada's booming trade with the U.S. wasn't really trade in the traditional sense of exchanging goods between "arms length" industrial entre-preneurs and competitors, it was the transfer of goods between U.S. factories and Canadian branch plants. Canada's industry was not so much a true *manufacturing* facility, it became an assembly facility for basic components manufactured elsewhere — mostly in America. While Canada's "industry" apparently grew by leaps and bounds during the post-World War II years,

Canada's *real* ability to produce products from start-to-finish *declined*.

But this did not seem to matter as long as employment was assured and Canadians remained prosperous. Unfortunately, these two conditions depended upon a factor entirely beyond Canadian control ... *the American economy had to remain healthy.*

* * * * * *

Napoleon once said that "history is the lie commonly agreed upon". In the case of our decade-long economic tragedy, the lie commonly agreed upon is that the bubble burst when the "Arabs" raised the price of oil in late 1973. This started the whole economic decline, according to the average Canadian's view of history, and began the spiral of inflation. The effect of oil on North American life and economics is readily understandable, and the fact that OPEC, quadrupled the price of oil within months during the winter of 1973-1974 was an apparently logical explanation for the troubles that followed.

The popularity of this "history" is due also to the fact that it is easier to blame someone else for one's troubles than blame oneself.

In spite of "the lie commonly agreed upon", North America signalled its economic decline more than two years before OPEC did its dirty deed.

James Laxer, in his analysis of contemporary economic problems (*Rethinking the Economy*, New Canada Publications, Toronto, 1983), offers an exact date for the "official" end of North America's post-World War II economic prosperity. On August 15, 1971 the Nixon administration in the United States announced a new economic order consisting of several unilateral policies:

1. *The convertibility of U.S. dollars into gold was ended,* which meant that foreigners (mostly central banks) holding U.S. dollars were holding mere paper.
2. *A 10 per cent surcharge on all imports was imposed.* It was an emergency measure.
3. *A new tax write-off program was extended to American*

> *industry*. The DISC (Domestic International Sales Corporations) scheme allowed substantial tax write-offs on products that American companies exported.

These Nixon moves caught Canada, and the rest of the developed world, by complete surprise. Every non-Communist industrialized nation complained bitterly to Washington ... Canada even sent a delegation to plead for an exemption under the 10% surcharge policy . . . but Nixon remained adamant.

As Laxer makes very clear, although the United States was able to make its unilateral policies stick within the Western World because of its economic and military clout, these policies were an admission of economic decline . . . they were intended to preserve and protect a huge, but obsolescent, industrial establishment.

America had a problem, and Nixon recognized it: the United States was losing its competitive edge over Western Europe and Japan. The handwriting had been on the wall for some time, and the more perceptive economic observers had been concerned for a few years, but the sheer size of America's industry had disguised the core disease from the average North American. By 1971 the disease had become visible to the Nixon administration and something had to be done about it.

In 1971 and 1972 the United States experienced a trade deficit for the first time in its post-war history. The decline has continued ever since.

> In 1970 the U.S. had a $2.6 billion surplus in its trade in manufactured products; in 1981 the country experienced a disastrous $27.8 billion deficit in its manufacturing trade.[1]

What has gone wrong?

Every Canadian (or American) can see what has gone wrong simply by looking around. The streets are filled with Japanese, German, French, Swedish and Italian automobiles ... most Canadians own one. Homes are filled with Japanese stereos and television sets, offices filled with Japanese, Dutch or German-manufactured data-processing equipment, time is told by Japanese digital watches, and vacation highlights captured with Japanese or German cameras.

In the beginning, back in the golden age of the post-war boom, the potential economic threat posed by Western Europe and Japan was not taken seriously. We were more apt to joke about these products of primitive industries trying to recover from wartime destruction. The only virtue of these products was that they were cheaper than North American products, but they were of inferior quality. People used to laugh at the Volkswagen "Beetles", slander Japanese transistor radios and "copies" of American TVs and cameras.

Now, of course, the joke is on us. Foreign design is acknowledged to be superior to North American engineering . . . and now the foreign products are not always cheaper.

The bottom line is that North American industry became complacent during the boom years and wakened to find itself obsolete. Nixon admitted that the alarm clock had gone off when he announced the unilateral American economic policies of August 15, 1971. They were all designed to protect American industry . . . which had once been the most competitive in the world.

It is worth returning to discuss the OPEC oil price hikes because they had a surprising aspect to them unsuspected by the average North American citizen. The fact is that Washington signalled OPEC in 1972 and 1973 that *an increase in the price of oil would be welcomed.* The reason for this is obvious, on reflection: the United States gets a significant amount of its oil from within its own borders . . . while Western Europe and Japan are almost totally dependent upon oil imported from OPEC countries. An increase in the OPEC price would (and did) hurt America's industrial competitors more than it hurt the United States.

Advisors to Nixon's administration recognized clearly enough that the problem wasn't OPEC, but the obsolete state of American industry. The average citizen, of course, was encouraged to believe that the "Arabs" were the cause of all the trouble.

When people are confronted with indisputable evidence of failure, a very human tendency is to try to blame it on someone else. Just as average citizens were encouraged to accept the fiction that the "Arabs" caused the basic economic decline, American (and Canadian) business executives are fond of saying that the economic deterioration has also been due to various things that have crippled good old-fashioned North American "free enterprise". They cite government interference in the form of anti-pollution legislation as an extra cost that competitive industry cannot afford. They cite the increased labour costs as a disadvantage to competitive industry. They site the added tax burdens imposed by governments to pay for social welfare programs as a load that keeps industry from being able to expand. They argue that government fiscal intervention in the economy prevents the "market system" from working.

Robert Reich's analysis of the North American industrial decline demonstrates that the real cause of economic recession involves none of these things in any significant way. The real cause of North American economic decline involves fundamental mistakes made by industrial executives themselves.

Reich teaches business and public policy at Harvard University and was formerly the Director for Policy Planning with the Federal Trade Commission in the United States. His 1983 book, *The Next American Frontier* is based on his own analysis and studies of his colleagues at the Harvard business school. It cannot be said that Reich and his colleagues are radicals or socialists. They mold the heart and soul of America's capitalist economy. What Reich has to say about U.S. executive decision-making is not very flattering. He doesn't pull his punches. According to Reich, *U.S. economic decline is due almost entirely to the incompetence of America's top business executives.*

Reich deals briefly with the mythic excuses so often voiced by North American "free enterprise" spokesmen ... and Laxer repeats the gist of Reich's analysis at some length in *Rethinking the Economy*. The facts and figures are detailed in Reich's and Laxer's books. The *facts* are that West European and Japanese industry have *higher* relative labour costs, *stricter* and more costly pollution control legislation to contend with, operate within nations with *more* "socialization" and direct government fiscal influence ... *and still manage to beat North American industry in the competition game.* Further, energy and raw materials costs are relatively higher for West European and Japanese industry because a much greater percentage of both have to be imported than is the case for North American industry.

The real problem, Reich argues, was two decades of complacency within the production base of the economy.

The gigantic industrial establishment created during World War II in the United States was taken for granted, and it was assumed that it was so awesome in size and so efficient that its superiority was assured. The business task was to fine-tune the management of this gigantic productive apparatus in order to extract maximum profit from it. Accordingly, top executives were recruited from the legal and accounting disciplines rather than from the engineering or production-oriented disciplines. Reich gives figures for this change in "executive origin" within American industry, as compared with the case in contemporary West European and Japanese industry, and the difference between them is clear.

These legal-accounting executives made their decisions on the basis of short-term profitability. This was the criterion by which they were judged and by which their reputations were made. Certain vital aspects of viable productivity were ignored because they did not contribute to short-term profit and, in fact, represented immediate expenditures with only the potential for future profits. Since top executives moved around increasingly and their careers with any one company steadily decreased in length, these executives avoided approving programs that meant immediately increased overhead (which decreased profit during their tenure) but which might bear fruit long in the future (for which someone else was likely to get the credit).

As a result, "research and development" was neglected ... programs of plant modernization were shelved or postponed. New products were developed less often, not only because "research and development" was expensive, but also because new products would displace existing product inventory and waste money. It proved more "cost effective" to re-package existing products and to sell them through increased advertising.

Inevitably, the superiority of North American industry became much more apparent than real. The industrial apparatus of Western Europe and Japan, having been re-built since World War II, was inevitably newer and more efficient. Emphasis upon top management with production and manufacturing experience ensured a regular upgrading of products and manufacturing techniques. Then, because of the engineering representation in top management, West European and Japanese industries were more responsive to the introduction of new manufacturing techniques and new product development. The West Europeans and Japanese realized that increasingly skilled labour was necessary to exploit "high technology" manufacturing and they developed social structures and job security to retain and educate workers . . . an unjustifiable added overhead in the view of North American executives. Why spend money to train workers who might leave and work for a competitor? Why bear the added costs of job security programs and policies when workers could always be found?

This is a greatly, abbreviated outline of the evolution that Reich describes in detail, but bottom line is that North American industry, and society, have become primitive in contrast to the rapid development forced on Western Europe and Japan. North American business and industry cannot compete. According to Reich, an outmoded productive apparatus is not the only problem . . . outmoded ideas and rhetoric about "free enterprise" may be an even bigger problem because they keep the *real* problem from being identified and solved. As long as "free enterprise" is somehow equated with "profitability" in a very short-sighted way, then business executives (and their corporations) can delude themselves that they are successful and competitive *as long as they turn a profit.* And, more important, as long as business appears to be "successful" then the North American society as a whole can continue to delude itself that there is nothing wrong with the basic social and industrial order. In fact, there's even an emotional pull toward the traditional "free enterprise" type of values based on this short-term "success" at "turning a profit". This, according to Reich is the source of *the new conservatism* that brought Reagan and Mulroney to power. Given the threat to North American industry, it seemed almost patriotic to support the new conservatism.

The problem is that the success and profitability of North American business is largely illusory. There are many ways of showing a profit and therefore succeeding . . . if you're an executive with an accounting or legal background. Since the majority of North American top executives do have a legal or accounting background, the last 15 years of North American business have witnessed many creative ways of "showing a profit" ... on paper. Reich describes these antics as "merger mania" and fully covers the way in which the "acquisition of assets" becomes "profit" and success ... *even though not a penny of real wealth has actually been created through increased industrial production.*

Needless to say, merger mania reached out-patient proportions among executives as they struggled to keep themselves deluded about the real competitive facts of life ...

> "Merger mania" as it has been called, has become the consuming passion of American business management. In 1978 alone, eighty mergers took place in the United States involving companies with assets of at least $100 million. the following year nearly a hundred such mergers occurred. These amalgamations involved the transfer of $20 billion from owner to owner. This was a far more interesting game for American managers to play than learning to compete with the Japanese and Europeans in a world of ever shrinking markets in relation to industrial capacity.[2]

Merger mania is a lucrative malady for those executives, accountants and lawyers involved in negotiating the transactions. They are paid in real money, and sometimes on the basis of some percentage of the transaction's value. This money is paid out of corporate profits which might better be spent in upgrading production facilities or in research and development. Naturally, except for the employment of a few lawyers, accountants and their assistants, the exchange of all these billions and the paper profits do not result in increased employment or increased production.

The American economy has been hit very hard by European and Japanese competition since 1971 ... but Canada was devastated. Not only did the branch-plant type of economy magnify the impact of North American industrial decline, but also the nature of our American-dominated economy made Keynesian prescriptions for recovery counter-productive.

It may be helpful to recall the three policies announced by the

Nixon administration on August 15, 1971 because they struck at the fragility of the Canadian economy ...

1. *The convertibility of U.S. dollars into gold was ended,* which meant that foreigners (mostly central banks) holding U.S. dollars were holding mere paper.
2. *A 10 per cent surcharge on all imports was imposed.*
3. *A new tax write-off program was extended to American industry.* The DISC (Domestic International Sales Corporations) scheme allowed substantial tax write-offs on products that American companies exported.

The first policy, ending the convertibility of U.S. dollars into gold, began the era of galloping inflation in the post-war Western World. At the risk of distortion through over-simplification, this policy made U.S. dollars "worthless" because they could no longer be exchanged for a given quantity of a precious commodity as had formerly been guaranteed. The worth of the dollar became a reflection of one's confidence in the U.S. economy and, since that economy was starting to face serious competition for the first time in post-war history, confidence in its value decreased. More money was demanded in exchange for commodities because of this lack of confidence. Since the U.S. dollar had been the dominant currency, its value dropped in relation to the currencies of other nations, notably in relation to the currencies of Western Europe and Japan. This *relative devaluation* of the U.S. dollar with respect to other currencies made it easier for U.S. companies to sell their products abroad and made it harder for foreigners to sell their products in America.

Today, of course, we have the reverse situation — an increasingly strong US. dollar and low inflation — in which American companies are finding it difficult to export. This situation was created solely by increased government spending, and lower taxation, creating a budget deficit of hundreds of billions of dollars per year, as well as unprecendented foreign trade deficits. These deficits, if continued for many more years, threaten to completely undermine the U.S. economy — and consequently the economies of all Western industrial nations .... especially Canada's.

But lack of confidence in the stability of the world economy caused *all* currencies to lose value compared to their value before Nixon ended the convertibility of the U.S. dollar into gold. The inflationary spiral had begun, which was accelerated by the OPEC oil price increases of 1973-1974, and which has continued ever since.

The second Nixon policy of August 15, 1971, the 10% surcharge on all imported goods, was designed to raise the price of imported goods in order to discourage Americans from buying them. Since the United States was Canada's largest export market, this move by Nixon was a serious blow to the Canadian economy.

But the third Nixon policy, the DISC program, demonstrated the extreme vulnerability of Canada's branch-plant economy. DISC gave tax write-off on products exported by American companies ... it was a U.S. government incentive to stimulate exports.

Canadian subsidiary operations of U.S. manufacturers had largely become *assemblers* of components actually produced in American. DISC incentives stimulated this "trade" whereby U.S. manufactured goods flooded into Canada. The assembly aspect of production was not stimulated nearly so much as the manufacturing process. The result was that DISC stimulated employment in the United States much more than it stimulated employment in Canada.

DISC highlighted the disadvantages of the branch-plant economy at a time when inflation (caused by U.S. non-convertibility policy) and inhibition of Canadian exports to the U.S. (caused by Nixon's 10% surcharge policy) forced a desperate scrutiny of Canada's entire economic structure. In fact, however, the branch-plant "solution" to industrial growth had always been more apparent than real. It had been draining Canadian industrial potential for years, but disguised by visible employment and visible new industrial buildings. Branch-plants gave the visible illusion of employment and industrial growth. What was not seen so clearly by Canadians until the crisis of the 1970s was the invisible costs they'd always been paying. The whole idea of a subsidiary is that it will assemble what the "head office" manufactures. This is a bad bargain for the country in which the branch-plant is located ...

The consequence of the forced selling of American produced goods in the Canadian market through branch plants has been deindustrialization for Canada. The loss of industrial jobs has been staggering. In the early Seventies, the Harvard Business School estimated the net U.S. gain/Canadian loss as a direct result of this at 300,000 jobs.[3]

In short, without a branch-plant economy Canada would have 300,000 more jobs than at present.

The Liberal "quick-fix" to produce industry magically back in the late 1940s and early 1950s has backfired tragically. The original idea of attracting American investment was to retain a free enterprise economy for Canada, to avoid the alternative of accepting public/government investment in industrial development ("socialism", "nationalization"). The irony would be comic if it were not so tragic. Forty years after the quick fix to save free enterprise, Canada's economy is anything but free. In fact, we are so fettered that we cannot even begin our own economic recovery.

The branch-plant economy confronts Canada with something even more serious than the loss of 300,000 jobs ... it turns Keynesian economics upside down.

Keynesian economics worked, and worked very well, in regulating more or less steady economic growth during the post-war boom years. There was no serious inflation, there was no runaway expansion that could lead to a collapse. The boom-and-bust cycle of capitalism seemed to have been tamed. Unfortunately, the Keynesian model was based on the assumption of a closed system ... or at least, on the assumption of a reasonably insulated system. It worked well for the U.S. system with its huge productive capacity (back in the good old days) and huge domestic market. It worked well in European countries where there were substantial domestic markets and balanced trade with a number of different neighbors.

And it even worked well for Canada ... *so long as Canada was effectively a part of the U.S. economy and there were no great barriers discriminating against Canadian imports and favouring American exports.* The situation changed in the 1970s with the unilateral implementation of Nixon's policies of August 15, 1971 and with the culmination of the branch-plant economy in

Canada. Nixon's policies erected barriers against any real trade, on an equitable basis, between Canada and the U.S. and, at the same time, branch-plant type "trade" destroyed Canadian economic independence.

Keynesian economic theory was never designed to cope with this sort of situation.

The Keynesian idea is basically simple. If the economy slows down and there is unused industrial capacity and, therefore unemployment, the situation can be reversed by an outside infusion of money. If people are provided with money they will spend a certain percentage of it on goods. This added demand will stimulate production. Stimulated production will increase employment. Employment will provide income and the economy is moving again.

Conversely, if the economy starts moving too quickly, with demand (and money) exceeding the supply of goods — an outside source can step in and subtract money from the economy. This discourages demand and prevents inflation.

In both cases, of course, this outside source is the government. It can create infusions of capital during times of unemployment by social programs like unemployment insurance, welfare and tax incentives to manufacturers. It can subtract money in boom times, and slow down an overheated economy, by imposing additional taxes and by cutting back on social programs. In theory, the deficits incurred to stimulate a sluggish economy will equal the additional revenues obtained by extra-taxing of runaway economies.

In spite of 15 years of failure of this system within the Canadian economy, and the natural cynicism toward it bred in the hearts of free enterprisers in Canada, the Keynesian model does work admirably elsewhere . . . and has for years. One of the places where it first forked with most dramatic results, and where it has continued to work, happens to be in the "free enterprise" United States. The threat of a major disruptive post-war recession was most acute in the United States in the late 1940s, and simply because the U.S. had developed a gigantic wartime productive capacity which threatened to be "turned off" at the coming of peace. America's swords could not quickly be transformed into ploughshares and the transition to a peace-time economy was a frightening thought to soliders, workers, politicians and economists alike.

The solution was easy enough, according to the Keynesian model. Everyone pretended that the war was still on, and that only the enemy had changed. The militarism formerly directed against Nazi Germany and Imperial Japan was re-directed ... toward the Soviet Union and the international communist menace. It was the time of the "Cold War" ... and it assisted a partial return to a peace-time economy. The government provided infusions of capital, not to consumers through social programs as is the case in more "socialist" countries, but to manufacturers of arms. But the economic result is precisely the same according to the Keynesian model ... an artificial stimulus to the economy provided by government. In the U.S., military spending performs a part the Keynesian role of economic stimulus, and does to this day.

This is not to say that the Cold War was completely artificial and that there was no reason to fear a Soviet-Communist menace. The Soviets gobbled up Eastern Europe and threatened Berlin and performed various other antics that partly justified the U.S. response ... but not the extent of it. And there is legitimate reason today to wonder how much military Keynesianism by the U.S. has contributed to international tension.

Keynesian economics has worked in the States, and in other countries, but it has not worked since 1971 in Canada. The reason is that *The Keynesian model cannot work in a branch-plant economy*. If a branch-plant economy like Canada's slows down, as did happen in 1971, then the government *should* apply the Keynesian correction ... the government should provide an infusion of capital. Because Canada is not particularly militarist, this capital is infused among would-be consumers in the form of welfare, unemployment insurance, make-work projects, etc. They proceed to spend a significant percentage of this money on goods and this should stimulate the Canadian economy.

But it cannot ... for the simple reason that the goods these people purchase are largely manufactured elsewhere. They are either "pure" imports, mostly from the United States, or they are "partial" imports in the form of branch-plant goods manufactured elsewhere, mostly in the United States, and merely assembled in Canada.

The money, therefore, is diverted. Expenditures by the Canadian government do not stimulate the Canadian industrial sector, the expenditures end up stimulating the U.S. industrial sector.

No matter how much money is infused into a branch-plant economy, it gets siphoned away to stimulate the parent economy that manufactures the consumer products.

The situation seems hopeless ... but it is even worse.

In the Canadian economy, Keynesian infusions of stimulus capital not only fail to activate the economy, *but produce inflation*, by increasing the monetary supply and a rise in the price of goods and is therefore counter-productive. It can do nothing about stimulating *real* economic growth because the *real* economy is elsewhere. It can do very little to encourage real employment, although it might give a boost to the assembly and service sectors of the branch-plant economy ... in which case the government finds itself subsidizing the operations of the parent economy to an even greater greater degree than merely providing consumers with spending power. Finally, added to the unemployment and drain of money, the Keynesian model applied to a branch-plant economy produces inflation.

However, the government cannot let its people starve. It must keep supplying even an inadequate minimum to the unemployed and those who cannot join the work force. In order to do this, the government must borrow money when it runs out of any surplus it may have enjoyed. The interest on the debt becomes yet another burden created by the branch-plant "solution" and, as the national debt rises, this additional cost becomes anything but negligible.

The Canadian crisis becomes completely understandable. Why do we have high unemployment? Why can we not get our economy moving? Why is our currency devalued? Why are we spending so much, and going so heavily into debt, with no apparent improvement? Why can't "the government" do anything ...?

It is all terribly simple. We do not control out own economy. We are paying the price for the comfortable "quick fix" branch-plant solution of creating a *visible* economy like magic.

* * * * * *

In his *Rethinking the Economy*, James Laxer goes though this painful analysis in great detail, relying upon the assessment of U.S. economic decline provided by Robert Reich and others at Harvard. I have presented only the barest outline of Reich's and Laxer's work ... but enough, I hope, to show that this perspective of U.S. and Canadian economic crisis is hardly in the nature of a theory. It all makes sense, it fits the facts.

Laxer was primarily concerned with the NDP's response to Canada's current troubles. His purpose was to stimulate the NDP into a re-assessment of its economic policy, and also to stimulate an NDP re-assessment of the party's basic ideology.

As I understand Laxer's criticism of current NDP economic policy and basic ideology *in the light of world developments over the past 30-odd years*, he is saying two major things to his fellow democratic socialists:

1. Keynesian economic policy cannot work in Canada's uniquely branch-plant economy.
2. A trade union base is not suitable for a democratic socialist party in Canada.

We have dealt with Laxer's first point, but the second point also deserves some discussion. Laxer does not emphasize this second point in his book, presumably to avoid offending NDPers even more than his criticism of Keynesian Holy Writ, but he hints at it.

And it is impossible to follow up this hint without striking a blow against the very ideological foundation of Marxism. Perhaps Laxer realized this himself ... and chose to back off criticism of an even more sacred Holy Writ. He himself had been a radical Marxist, remember?

But it seems to me, if I am not doing Laxer an injustice, that he realized that North American trade unions are not automatically a "progressive" social element as Marxists *must* believe and as socialists are all too prone to believe. Laxer writes:

> Free collective bargaining on wages and salaries was the *raison d'être* of the Canadian labour movement. In the adversarial system to which they were accustomed, unions did not generally concern themselves with the well being of

whole sectors of the economy ... Instead they faced employers across the table to win the best possible money and benefits package for their members. As far as unions were concerned, the solution to inflation was collective bargaining. Unions would demand wages and salaries that kept their members ahead of the game, seeking COLAs (Cost of Living Allowances) to make sure their members did not suffer during the life of a contract.

Armed with their own solution to the problems of inflation (collective bargaining), most trade unionists did not see any problem with continuing to advocate the traditional Keynesian solutions to fight unemployment. The problem was unemployment, not inflation, labour leaders declared in a litany that was to become very familiar during the Seventies and early Eighties.

The NDP followed suit, at least on the federal level. Fight unemployment not inflation, NDP leaders declared repeatedly. Not only did this line of argument keep peace in the family with the CLC (Canadian Labour Congress), it also fitted well with the NDP's general economic views. Since the party cared more about consumer spending power as the key to full employment than it did about the health of the nation's industries, it was not particularly concerned that high domestic inflation would have harmful affects (sic) on Canada's international economic performance ...

A political analysis that does not deal with the problem of inflation and a political program that cannot counter its ravages can have only limited appeal. The majority of workers who fell behind inflation in the period cited above could be forgiven for believing the NDP had a "survival of the fittest" approach to people's incomes, in which those with strong bargaining power win and the others lose.[4]

That is as much as Laxer says in terms of trade union criticism, but it is clear that more far-reaching conclusions could be entertained without much difficulty.

In both their history and their voting patterns, North American trade unions have demonstrated no significant tendency toward changing society as a whole. Generally, the trade unions of North America have demonstrated only a determination to obtain a greater share of the "free enterprise" economic pie. One might go further, as Laxer hinted, and observe that trade unions have been committed to the policy of getting the *biggest possible share* of the economic pie with very little concern for other social sectors.

We may recall the union's stand on rural electrification in Tommy Douglas's CCF government . . .

North American trade unions have mostly behaved in precisely the same way that North American capitalist robber-barons have behaved, motivated by a "survival of the fittest" outlook. The occasional socially conscious expressions of the larger and more successful trade unions in North America must be placed, objectively, in the same class with the philanthropic foundations established by the more successful business tycoons . . . "let's contribute to society when we can afford to, when and it provides a tax benefit". Within this context, Canada's current NDP is on par with the Ford Foundation or Andrew Carnegie's Trust . . . and about as relevant as these philanthropic organizations in compelling basic social change. The trade unions of North America are not committed to any fundamental behavioural-economic reconstruction of society. On the contrary, they are adversarial *partners* in the North American system.

No one, besides the owners and executives themselves, have a great stake in the preservation of obsolescent North American industry than the trade unions who work as adversaries within it. Just as the management men in, say, the North American auto industry had a tough row to hoe, Laxer writes of the Canadian Auto Workers . . .

> The transportation equipment workers lost badly to inflation at the end of the Seventies and the beginning of the Eighties. This sector included the autoworkers (both organized and unorganized). The Canadian United Auto Workers, probably the most effective and ably led industrial union in the country, was fighting against the very difficult problems of failing auto markets and tough Japanese competition.[5]

Which, of course, were precisely the problems of U.S. automobile manufacturer executives. The executives protected themselves with high salaries and "golden parachutes" of company-paid benefits if they left under pressure of failure . . . just as the unions protected themselves with COLAs. But everybody was in the same fight — the fight to defend an obsolescent industry against foreign challenge. The trade unions, and the management people understood each other very well indeed. Was there any squawking about "big business-government" on the part of UAW men, or any squawking of "government intervention" on the part of Chrysler executives, when the U.S. government floated a complex series of loans to keep Chrysler from going belly-up ... "free enterprise" style? Of course not.

* * * * * *

Laxer's father had been a Communist and James Laxer himself had once been a fairly radical and doctrinaire Marxist during the Waffle era. In his *Rethinking the Economy* Laxer found himself criticizing certain basic ideological assumptions that social democrats had been holding since accepting The Great Compromise. It may not be at all surprising, but it is nontheless ironic, that Laxer's 1983 criticisms of NDP outlook and policy, were received with a good deal more appreciation by the "free enterprise" sector than by the NDP and organized labour.

Canada's "business newspaper", the *Globe and Mail*, ventured the opinion that Laxer's analysis was ... "A much-needed jolt of political energy."

But Denis McDermott, President of the Canadian Labour Congress, asked in irritation: "Who made *him* an expert on NDP policy?"

And Pauline Jewett, New Democratic Party MP from New Westminister-Coquitlam, said: "Mr. Laxer is out to lunch".

These NDP-labour responses are instinctual, deriving from *an outmoded doctrinaire ideology that never had any validity within North American Society*. It is an ideology that evolved from European Marxism and European class-consciousness and which was molded into the CCF and the modern NDP by David Lewis and other, mostly eastern, academics and philosophers like Frank Scott and Frank Underhill. This ideology assumes a "class struggle" between the owners of wealth and the workers who create it. Within this construct, trade unions *must* be "progressive" and socialist because theirs is a struggle to control the wealth they produce.

The classical and doctrinaire Marxist-evolved ideology did not concern itself with the health of the industrial and productive apparatus of a country except insofar as they wanted to ensure that the wealth derived from it was equitably distributed among the workers. It was assumed that the industrial/productive apparatus would always remain vital and competitive because of the greed and drive of the capitalist enterpreneurs. Modern NDP outlook is focused on distribution of wealth among the workers and unemployed of the industrial establishment, not the viability of the industrial establishment itself. Since things started to go wrong in the early 1970s, the NDP has consistently called for a "consumer-led recovery" ... the old Keynesian formula of stimulus by government infusions of money.

Nonetheless, some self-evident truths are starting to sink in, even into NDP policy. But the basic misconceptions upon which the party is based inevitably result in a certain degree of confusion and contradiction. In April 1985 the New Democratic Party unveiled a blueprint for economic recovery entitled "Canada Unlimited". It called for Keynesian medicine ... but also for stimulus to small business and co-operatives. "Canada Unlimited" proposed in part that:

> Deficit spending can be one of the most positive approaches to take to rebuild our economy.

And the program proposes a $1-billion net increase in the deficit ... which is not very much, as things are accounted now, and would not stimulate the country very much even if Keynesian economics worked in our branch-plant economy (which it doesn't). "Canada Unlimited" proposed an $850-million Community Initiatives Fund to help small business and co-operatives and a $400-million Youth Initiative Fund oriented toward jobs and job-training.

Commenting on "The NDP's blueprint" (*Globe and Mail*, April 10, 1985), Jeffrey Simpson wrote:

> Keynes is dead; long live Keynes.
> That could be the motto of the New Democratic Party's policy statement released yesterday.
> Entitled Canada Unlimited, the statement calls enemployment Canada's number one problem. But it can't quite decide what to do about the staggering federal deficit ...

... the statement proposes only a $1-billion net increase in the deficit, hardly enough to get the economy moving by pump-priming ...

Maybe this estrangement from conventional Keynes-ianism flows from a belated recognition of the staggering burden of the $35-billion deficit with its attendant interest payments and additions to the public debt. Or maybe it's part of the NDP's attempt to present a more contemporary public face. Either way, it's a step in the right direction.

Simpson acknowledges that the "broad strokes" of the NDP policy "don't add up", but that "some of the smaller touches might help an economy groaning under the weight of unaccept-ably high unemployment." Simpson, while drawing attention to the NDP's ideological-economic confusion, acknowledges a change for the better in the process of NDP policy-making:

The best part of Canada Unlimited is its openess. The task force travelled widely to hear from concerned Cana-dians about the economy. Rather than build theoretical castles in the sky, NDP MPs learned as they travelled. Their statement usefully pulls the NDP further from grandiose — and vote-losing — talk of centralized industrial strategies.

But the list of interlocutors is weighted heavily toward trade unionists, community groups and social-welfare lobby groups. These are normal constituencies for a left-of-centre party, but they by no means represent a complete cross-section of society.

Simpson is undoubtedly right when he observes that the NDP's attempts to hear the people's views, and reflect them in "Canada Unlimited" distanced the NDP from vote-losing *talk*. One can almost hear Tommy Douglas' whispered congratula-tions. He'd always insisted on developing policy from grassroots perceptions, not from theory.

But the fact of the matter is that the NDP has not distanced itself from vote-losing *ideology*. The basic confusion and contra-diction remains at the core of the party, and the voters know it.

The Ontario provincial election was held just one month after the release of the NDP's policy statement. "Canada Unlimited" was obviously unveiled in early April for use by NDP candidates campaigning for the May 2, 1985 election in Ontario.

Going into the election, the Tories held 72 seats, the Liberals 30 and the NDP 23. Just as in the crucial Ontario election of 1945 almost exactly 40 years before, the NDP looked forward to big gains. The Progressive Conservatives had just been split by a closely-contested leadership convention to decide on Bill Davis's replacement. Frank Miller, the eventual winner, had some internal fence-mending to do. Miller did not run a very good campaign and Davis, on exiting, had saddled the party with a controversial policy on separate school funding. In short, Miller and the "Big blue Machine" looked very vulnerable indeed in the two weeks before polling.

But, on election night, the big winner was not the NDP, but the Liberal Party. The voters of Ontario had repeated 1945 history. Instead of significant gains, the NDP picked up only 2 seats . . . for a total of 25. The Tories managed to hang on to a slim minority of 52 seats . . . but the Liberals surged from 30 to 48 seats to become the Official Opposition. Just like in 1945.

The NDP share of the popular vote was up, but not by much. the Liberal share of the popular vote was sharply up, and even exceeded the PC popular vote.

It was the same old story. The trade union vote did not go heavily to the NDP, but to one of the establishment parties (in this case, as in 1945, to the Liberal Opposition). The very many undecided and non-union voters who could have gone to the NDP did not do so. They split their vote between Tories and Grits with most of it going Liberal. They shied away from the NDP.

New Democrats have argued that there is no real difference between the Conservatives and the Liberals, that one is no real alternative for the other. Although this view has not *always* been valid (as with Diefendbaker and Joe Clark federally), it is quite obviously true in 1985. There's no real or significant difference between Liberals and Conservatives, and Canadian voters know this very well. They switch back and forth between the "white cats" and the "black cats" (as Douglas put it) for just one reason: to chastise a party that has been in power too long, to destroy patronage, corruption and complacency. This is usually expressed as "it's time for a change". Perhaps the only social sectors that are truly loyal to the two establishment parties are those that represent the industrial establishment: *management and unionized labour.* The rest of the electorate, which is a majority of voters, do not feel that they have a real alternative to the "white cats" and the "black cats" ... they simply don't trust the modern NDP. *It is the NDP that does not appear to be a viable alternative* to voters opposed to the Tories or Liberals. They sense in the NDP a conflict and confusion of identity that cannot be trusted ... and the voters are right.

Not long after the Ontario election of May 2, 1985 I spoke briefly with Martin Goldfarb about the NDP and the thesis of this book. I'm by no means sure that Goldfarb would agree with the perspective I propose for the NDP in later pages, but he emphatically agreed with one of my major points. Goldfarb's opinion polling has convinced him that Canadians will never flock to the NDP as long as it is officially affiliated with trade unions.

It is not that the Canadian people are "anti-union" because they're duped by "free enterprise" propaganda. It is not because they're "anti-Marxist" as good Capitalists. They distrust the trade unions, and the NDP's ideology for another, ironic reason ... *Marxist ideology is irrelevant and contradictory in 1985, and trade unions are a conservative ally of an outmoded economic system that desperately needs overhauling.*

Only the future will tell for sure if this is valid, but one can learn from the past, and it is significant that the people of Saskatchewan *did regard Tommy Douglas's CCF as a viable alternative to the black cats and white cats* ... but then Tommy Douglas and *his* CCF were not programmed by an inflexible and contradictory ideology. They were motivated by religious commitment and compassion. They wanted to create a more *humane* society and to alleviate unnecessary suffering while providing more opportunity for individual fulfillment. Theirs was a crusade against the sin of avarice and the suffering it caused. Douglas and his CCF retained flexibility of policy because they were not constricted by any doctrinaire method or system. There was no philosophical contradiction at the core of their CCF. They were able to make use of "socialist nationalization" where necessary, desirable or unavoidable. They were able to forge partnerships with "free enterprise" when that seemed to be the best or only answer. They worked for the welfare of farmers and industrial workers ... but did not hesitate to challenge union avarice when necessary. They were concerned about developing a viable economy by policies of capital investment ... using "free enterprise" capital when it could be obtained, using government and public investment when that was the final resort. In its concern with developing the productive apparatus of Saskatchewan, the CCF under Tommy Douglas departed from classical socialist ideology in a very profound way. It was a departure from Marxist doctrine that disturbed David Lewis.

Under Tommy Douglas, the CCF and NDP expressed a great deal of concern for the profile of The Great Compromise as sketched by the Liberals of Mackenzie King and, later, Trudeau. Douglas feared the future implications of American domination of Canada's industry. He felt that Canadian ownership, even if it must be government or public ownership ("nationalized"), of resource and energy industries was preferable to U.S. control. He preferred "nationalization" in these industries because practical considerations, not ideological "socialist" ones. First, Douglas realized that Canadian capitalist investors might decline to invest in long-term development projects in far-flung regions of the country where resources and energy sources might be. The Canadian private sector has never been noted for its investment courage. Then, "nationalization" was the only means of ensuring that energy and resource industries would remain in Canadian hands. Private industries can be bought and sold, control can be exchanged.

The CCF formed a government only in Saskatchewan in the immediate post-war years. In Ottawa and in other provinces its only power was moral. The CCF could not make policy in such a situation, it could only plead for policies that would benefit Canadian economic development in the long run.

The first clash came between Douglas and C.D. Howe over the Trans-Canada Pipeline issue. It was a resource and energy facility that involved the entire nation. Howe, who had worked closely with U.S. industry during World War II on defence production, wanted a rather curious affirmation of "free enterprise". The most difficult stretch of the pipeline, and the least profitable, passed through northern Ontario ... and the private sector didn't want to build it. Howe proposed that the government should pay for this unprofitable section ... and then that the pipeline be turned over to the private sector! In short, the Canadian people were to pay 95% of the pipeline's cost but would not "own" it or control it. Surely, that is the worst of both worlds of socialism vs. capitalism. But Howe saw nothing wrong with it. He staunchly supported "free enterprise", and was even willing to subsidize it with taxpayer money, so long as final ownership remained in private hands. Tommy Douglas could only argue that Saskatchewan would co-operate in building the pipeline on a Canadian-owned basis. But Douglas was rebuffed by C.D. Howe. The pipeline was eventually passed into private ownership with Home Oil having the major share in it.

The next clash on the subject of national energy and industry policy took place under more favourable circumstances for the NDP in 1973. There was a Liberal minority government under Pierre Trudeau and the NDP held the balance of power. Douglas, as NDP energy critic (David Lewis had become leader) demanded that Trudeau establish a Canadian-owned petroleum company to undertake exploration, production and distribution of Canadian oil and gas. Douglas demanded that one of the existing private oil companies operating in Canada be "acquired" for the purpose. Or else ... the NDP would withdraw its support in Parliament and force an election. The next day (Thursday, December 6, 1973) Trudeau rose in the Commons to announce the creation of Petrocan. As a result, Canadians have at least one small finger in their own energy-resource pie.

In their concern with industrial development, Douglas and his CCF colleagues did not act according to doctrinaire Marxist-socialist ideology which, under the tenets of The Great Compromise, leaves industrial development to the capitalists and concerns itself only with extracting from industry a share of the wealth for workers. Douglas realized that industrial development must be a Canadian priority, and he feared the future repercussions of the Liberals' branch-plant solution.

Even in Saskatchewan, all voters did not support the CCF by any means. Many preferred black cats or white cats. But everyone did know that Douglas's CCF was a completely different sort of political creature. It was a real and viable alternative. In Saskatchewan, an overwhelming majority of the electorate became convinced that Douglas's CCF represented their interests, and it seems that they were not deceived.

The modern NDP is a grey creature. It's visible image is the grey that must result from mixing black and white, that must result from mixing opposing and antithetical components and philosophies: simple human compassion, Marxist doctrine and historical perspective, the "free-enterprise" and "survival of the fittest" outlook of organized labour.

All across Canada the electorate of Mouseland is wary of this grey creature. The suspicion is that it might not be a mouse at all, but some even more destructive kind of cat.

Chapter Six

Crisis of Clarity:

Elections 1988

When people realize that they are being threatened, their first reactions are automatic: they retreat to some familiar position that is believed to be strong and secure; they try to identify the threat according to their abilities of perception; they take what they consider to be appropriate action to neutralize the threat as they perceive it.

These automatic first reactions may, or may not, prove to be successful in dealing with the threat. There can be misapprehensions all along the chain of reaction which lead to wrong decisions. The supposedly secure position may, in fact, be vulnerable. Perceptions may be distorted so that the threat is wrongly identified. The actions decided upon may be inadequate or even counter-productive. If the threat is successfully neutralized at all, success is not likely to have come because of the first automatic responses. Successful neutralization of the threat is likely to require changes of initial position, fine-tuning of perception and a variety of actions until the right combination of everything removes the threat at last.

The first automatic reactions are common to all of humanity and are probably instinctual behaviour much older than humanity. Everyone is prone to them, whether "socialist" or "capitalist", and these automatic responses are most likely to lead to errors in confronting threats efficiently.

In Canada, the Liberal Party's response to the coming of peace after World War II involved a hasty automatic response of this sort in constructing the Canadian version of The Great Compromise. The perceived threat was loss of political power to the CCF and/or social disruption because of a transition to peacetime economy. The immediate Liberal response was, on one hand, to adopt CCF social programs but, on the other hand, to reject the CCF policy for creating a viable peace-time economy by using public investment to develop industrialization. The Liberal automatic response to the need for creating an industrial economy was to attract American investment instead. It was based on a misapprehension about what constituted "free enterprise". Canada's economy ended up being anything but free.

When the recession of the early 1970s deepened to crisis proportions, the NDP and the Liberals (both parties being aware of the Keynesian aspect of The Great Compromise) agreed in applying Keynesian capital infusions to stimulate the economy out of recession. This did not work, for reasons outlined earlier, and the Liberals realized this clearly. They may have even understood why the Keynesian cure wasn't working. They continued running huge deficit budgets simply because they had no choice. Even if the Keynesian prescription wasn't working, the Liberal government couldn't let the unemployed starve. In following this hopeless economic policy, the Lberals nonetheless revealed themselves to be less confused than the NDP. The Liberal government continued to apply Keynesian stimulus, not in any real expectation that it would work, but for reasons of human welfare and because they had no political choice. They could only hope to hang on (accepting huge deficits) in the hope that the U.S. economy would improve its health. The NDP, by contrast, suffered from the misconception that Keynesian economics *must* be a familiar, secure and strong ideological position. The NDP (until April 1985) continued to demand massive government spending to produce the "consumer-led recovery". Theirs was an automatic response based on misconception.

Both Robert Reich and James Laxer have concluded that the spirit of "new conservatism" in contemporary North America is also an automatic response to the threat of economic decline. This "new conservatism", too, is characterized by misconceptions. Nonetheless, it brought Ronald Reagan to the White house in the United States and it brought Mulroney to power in Canada.

The "new conservatism" is, in essence, no more misguided than the NDP's refusal to abandon Keynesian economics in the 1970s, but it has the potential for resulting in a great deal more human suffering and lack of fulfillment than the NDP's misconceptions if only because the "new conservatives" are in power and the NDP is not. The "new conservatism" has the potential for causing greater disaster than even the Liberal structuring of the Canadian Great Compromise 40 years ago. Liberal mistakes and misconceptions back in the late 1940s merely had the effect of consigning Canada to the future miseries of a branch-plant economy, but the "new conservatism" can determine the social evolution of the entire North American continent for decades to come — if, indeed, we survive that long.

This "new conservatism" is, in reality, the economics of obsolescence and the politics of decline cloaked in brave, defiant and misleading rhetoric. Stripped of grandiloquent appeals to patriotism and grandiloquent praises of "free enterprise", *it is a desperate attempt to turn North America into a protected and isolated preserve for an obsolete industrial apparatus and the society it supports.*

With the landslide election of Brian Mulroney on September 4, 1984, this "new conservatism" has become a Canadian-American alliance. The intention is to create continental trade and energy policies that will preserve the obsolete industrial status quo. Obviously, many people in Canada and the United States are disposed to co-operate in this endeavour, which is why Reagan and Mulroney got elected, but the prime defenders of the obsolete structure are the "capitalists" who own and operate it and the trade unions who depend upon it.

Unfortunately for everyone, the "smokestack industries" of the outmoded American industrial apparatus have other drawbacks besides being unable to compete against the more evolved industries of Western Europe and Japan. They created a society that placed little value on social and human development, and have exhibited no evolution toward worker participation and education. It is a primitive and pyramidal industrial system with managers at the top, foremen in the middle and workers at the bottom. It is inflexible in both human and production terms. That was once the great strength of the American industrial apparatus — mass production of rather crudely engineered products using relatively unskilled labour — but that profile, so successful in the 1950's and 1960s, has become a liability. Robert Reich is concerned about the kind of society that has been created by this pyramidal industrial model. He considers the "next American frontier" to be the challenge of evolution into a more educated and flexible industry and society able to compete with the Europeans and Japanese.

But if the "new conservatives" are successful in preserving the "smokestack" industrial society, Americans will not rise to the challenge of social evolution and will not cross Reich's frontier.

Aside from the larger social considerations, these smokestack industries have blighted the landscape and polluted the environment. If the challenge of evolution is shirked by the "new conservatives", then the quality of North American environment will continue to deteriorate.

The smokestack industries never employed the most under-privileged segments of U.S. society except in the meanest poverty. There was no civic ethos which inspired the notion of using profits to make cities habitable. If the outmoded industrial system is to be preserved, then a significant portion of American people, especially minorities, will continue to exist near the poverty line and continue to inhabit decaying urban slums.

U.S. industry has always been based on military production to a much greater extent than most people realize. Aside from production earmarked for America's own defence, armaments have become an important export product category. Arms have become even more important to the U.S. economy since the start of European and Japanese industrial competition because armaments are a product category in which U.S. technology remains supreme. The Japanese produce virtually no armaments, and no European country can compete with American economies of scale. Then, except for certain categories of weapons, much military equipment remains simple, robust and primitive — ideal for continued "smokestack" production which was created by World War II to begin with. As the U.S. was increasingly hurt by foreign competition in the product categories of consumer goods, America responded by exporting ever greater quantities of armaments. Weapons have become the U.S. economy's *single most important export product category.*

According to the U.S. Defence Security Assistance Agency, U.S. arms exports totalled $946-million in the fiscal year 1970 . . . but jumped to $10.5-*billion* in in the fiscal year 1974, a ten-fold increase during America's export drive announced by Nixon first on August 15, 1971. U.S. arms exports presently top $20-billion annually.

Flooding the world with armaments can only further destabilize an already critical situation which affects everyone's security. But it is profitable. It is about the only means of "export retaliation" available to the American economy.

If the obsolescent industries are to be preserved, arms manu-facture and export must continue to play a crucial role in the economy of the "new conservatives". Weapons manufacture can easily be harnessed to the psychology of "patriotism" and the defence of "free enterprise". I remember one personal experience which captured the essence of this "new conservative" psychological matrix. In February 1983 I returned from England after a business trip and had a stop-over at Boston's Logan International Airport. A group of unemployed young men were demonstrating with placards and American flags. Messages on the placards read: "To Hell With Foreign Aid" and "Laser Weapons Mean Jobs" (referring to Reagon's so-called "Star Wars" defence program).

None of this paints a very pretty picture for the future of North America. If the "new conservatism" gets its way, the population of the continent will be regimented into a sort of "industrial feudalism" within a stagnant society, a polluted environment, decayed cities and increasing militarism to justify it all. Most will live in deepening poverty except for those lucky privileged vassals who happen to belong to powerful trade unions that helped to create the system and are an integral part of it.

The picture is worse for Canada.

Brian Mulroney's "successful surrender" to the existing Canadian predicaments must result in acceptance of Canada's branch-plant status. At best, Mulroney can only hope to get the system functioning again. Quite obviously, in line with the ideal of providing protection for obsolescent industry within North America, the answer will be continental trade and energy-resource agreements. Such plans have already been announced — Mulroney's "Blockbuster" Canada-U.S. trade arrangements announced in March and April 1985 and still being negotiated.

Whatever the rhetoric, such agreements can have only one result: *Canadian resources will become available to fuel the continent's industrial system*, which means the American industrial apparatus. We have nothing else to offer, after all, but our resources. And in return the Americans will agree to invest in Canada again.

Unfortunately, the branch-plant economy will work the way it always has. The system will stimulate American employment more that Canadian employment, the system will increasingly make Canada a captive market for U.S. imports. The branch-plant economy, even if it operates at full capacity, cannot employ

Canada's expanded work force. Even with renewed and un-regulated American investment and activity, many Canadians can never find secure or equitable employment within the satellite economic system. They are destined to remain outcasts subsisting at the poverty level with no hope of anything better.

If Mulroney's "continental" initiatives are successful, and there's no reason to think they won't be, then "private sector" will appear to have been successful and "free enterprise" will appear to have been vindicated. That being the case, social programs wil be cut back. The *appearance* will be a vital economy, but the reality will be an economy that cannot sustain all Canadians Those at the bottom, and there will be many millions of them, will be characterized as those who just couldn't hack it in a free enterprise economy. They will be castigated and abandoned.

But life will not be bad for those who manage to find a niche in the revitalized satellite economic system. These people will number among them large and well-organized trade unions, top and middle executives and the numerous categories of clerical and service people. *The trade union members will be the most secure because they can protect their position by collective action.*

The least secure people will be those non-unionized and "white collar" workers who are not organized, have no specific skills and who can be easily replaced from the vast pool of unemployed people at the base of the feudal industrial pyramid: salesclerks, unorganized factory workers or workers with weak unions in non-primary industries, middle and lower management people, junior and intermediate technical personnel. These people will be very careful and anxious indeed to keep their niche in the "new conservative" economic order because they will have the awful example, when the social programs are cut back, of what it means to be replaced. The vulnerable ones represent the *majority* of Canadians:

> Most Canadians, about 70 per cent of wage and salary earners, work in the so-called service sector of the economy. They work for banks, insurance companies, merchandising operations, and in education, health care and private and public administration. Many of them work for govern-ments.

Such people often find it difficult to believe that the fate of their sector of the economy depends very much on the health of commodity production. But it is so. If they work in the merchandising of products, their relation to the commodity-producing sector is obvious. If they work for banks or insurance companies, the relationship is very direct. The financial institutions of Canada have always had their base in the nation's commodity production. For educators and health care professionals, the relationship is less direct, but nonetheless very real. Without the surplus generated in goods production, the revenues to sustain the educational and health care systems would not be there.[1]

This is all very obvious, and most Canadians *know* it. If 70% of Canadians are employed in the "so-called service sector" of the economy they are acutely aware that their jobs are dependent upon the actual goods-production done somewhere else. Presently, their jobs (if they have one) and their welfare (if they are unemployed) are "artificially" provided by huge government deficits in one form or another. If the formula of the "new conservatives" becomes established, a *few* more of these people may find employment . . . but the unemployed will be much worse off.

It is important to realize that the surrender to Canada's predicament as personified by Brian Mulroney's "new conservatism" cannot, by definition, result in a truly expanding and independent economy. Beneath the very visible bustle of a revitalized economy, and beneath the very visible evidence of minimally-increased employment (and *any* increase in employment will appear to be a victory), there lies the implacable reality: *the Canadian economy cannot truly grow.* Under a revitalized branch-plant system, which Brian Mulroney wants to produce, Canadian small business will have a decreasing chance of survival. They will have to compete against multinational corporations which have been encouraged to undertake increased investment and activity in Canada. Home-grown Canadian small business had a hard time *before.* Under the "new conservatism", despite the rhetoric, Canadian enterprise will hardly take root before it is trampled by U.S. competition. Since small business provides more jobs than major corporations on a per-company basis, Canada's employment prospects will be further reduced.

It is my own view that most Canadians see all of this very

clearly indeed. I venture the opinion that Brian Mulroney's landslide victory of September 4, 1984 presents all Canadians with a "crisis of clarity". Are we to become economic serfs within the "new conservatism" and its establishment of a sort of feudal industrialism to protect an outmoded productive apparatus? Are we to scramble for a niche in the new order to come under these "new conservatives"? ... or is there an alternative?

My own opinion is that there *is* an alternative. It is an alternative that should have been offered by the New Democratic Party. It is an alternative that might not have attracted a majority of the electorate presently, but might have attracted a significant minority of them. It is an alternative that might attract a significant minority by the time the election of 1988 rolls around. By then, we will all have seen what the "new conservatism" *really* means ...

And what is this alternative? It is a vision of a society based on fearless humanism, not inflexible methodology. It is a crusade, not against any supposed religious adversary, *but against whatever would seek to fetter the aspirations of responsible people.* Only the New Democratic Party could conceivably offer this alternative, because both the Grits and Tories are fearful and cynical dependents upon an obsolescent economy and society.

But the NDP has failed to offer this alternative because of ideological confusion.

* * * * * *

I referred briefly before to my interest in "sociobiology", or how human behavior can be explained in terms of adaptation to the environment. Much of this knowledge has been gathered by observing animal behavior and adapting it to human situations. One such area is the phenomenon of "territoriality" or the inherent instinct of animals to "claim" territory and defend it. A bird might claim a particular bough of a tree, or stretch of telephone line, "sing" to claim it, and chase any other bird away from it. Although this sort of behavior had been noted for many years among observant naturalists, no one knew what to make of it. The best guesses were that this "territory" must have some economic significance — maybe enough territory was claimed and defended to ensure an adequate food supply. Many kinds of animals indulged in this behavior: antelopes, fish, birds, primates. Naturalists watched, and took notes, but were not much the wiser concerning this curious behavior.

Meanwhile, other naturalists discovered that some species, although they didn't seem to claim and defend an actual chunk of geographical space, did seem to claim and defend "social territory". Konrad Lorenz observed jackdaws — a kind of European crow — for years, and he was able to prove that these birds competed for status within their flocks. Higher status meant first access to food, favourable roosts, and sexual partners. Many animals exhibited the drive to compete for "social territory": barnyard hens, many kinds of primates, predators like lions and wolves in their prides and packs.

Further, scientists also made the discovery that territorality could take many different forms, some of them very complicated. Primates, or the more advanced monkeys and apes, sometimes exhibited territorial behavior in two ways simultaneously. Within a group of primates, males compete for status in much the same way as in jackdaw society, but with one difference. Most social primates are not monogamous. A troop of baboons does not divide itself into pairs like a flock of jackdaws. In primate society, the highest-ranking males have priviledged access to food, shelter and females on a "frequency-by-status" basis . . . all the females constituting a sort of shared harem enjoyed by the males of rank.

While this is going on within a group, the group itself will compete with other groups in the assertion and defence of spatial territory. This animal warfare is led by the ranking males. Successful groups can dominated and absorb others to create "monkey empires" although this is a relatively rare occurrence. The more usual situation is a jostling confusion of "monkey nations", all mutually aggressive, whose fortunes wax and wane without absolute decline, fall and absorbtion.

Needless to say, these observations of animal behavior did not prove to be very popular among 1960's-type "liberals". Human warfare was not only mirrored in the animal world, it was exhibited in its most complex and human-like form by those monkeys and apes most closely related to mankind. If we evolved from a common ancestor not too many million years ago, then maybe warfare was older than man ... and much older than capitalism! Then, it seemed as if greed and biological elitism were not only much older than capitalism and mankind, but were biologically necessary to ensure "the survival of the fittest". This was, of course, what the capitalists and free-enterprisers had always been saying — and it seemed as though they had fact on their side.

It did not take long before "conservative" social philosophers jumped on all this behavioural data to defend the ideals of competition-through-capitalism, "free enterprise", elitism and "survival of the fittest", not only as a natural order *but as a necessary one* if the viability of the race was to be preserved. The most prominent among these, or the most successful because of his evocative writing style, was Robert Ardrey. He made the rather esoteric and complex field of "new biology" not only understandable to average readers, but exciting. Ardrey's *The Social Contract* (1970) and The *Territorial Imperative* (1971) explained all of this new research in fascinating detail, and Ardrey did not fail to underline the apparently obvious and inescapable lessons for modern society. *The Social Contract* and *The Territorial Imperative* were instant best-sellers in original hardcover, and sold hundreds of thousands in mass-market paperback reprint. The Western World's reading public got another dose of factual, exciting (and titillating) "new biology" in the form of Desmond Morris's *The Naked Ape* (1967) which perforce supported Ardreyesque arguments.

I was, and am, enthralled by and envious of Robert Ardrey's sheer writing ability. His *plea*, for it is nothing less than that, for the preservation of biological elitism in contemporary society makes the final pages of *The Social Contract* one of the most moving passages of popular scientific literature ever written.

These were the prophets of the "new conservatism", biologists like Ardrey and Morris. They have an apparently unassailable justification for the "free-enterprise" system and for competition based, in the end, on natural order and survival necessity, not comparative economic merit of opposing systems of ideology. The biologists' books were continental bestsellers.

The timing of these biological books could not have been

better for the groundswell of the "new conservatism" in North America. *The Naked Ape* (1967), *The Social Contract* (1970) and *The Territorial Imperative* (1971) came just when needed to support the spurious Nixonian defence of "free enterprise" as represented by the *protectionist* measures of August 15, 1971. Coupled with military sabre-rattling and "free-enterprise" rhetoric, Nixon's aggressive assertion of North American economy seemed allied to the "new biology" in a way that made sense to the average person.

However . . .

Just as Nixonian measures of August 15, 1971 were assertions disguising weakness, the assertions of Robert Ardrey disguised a weakness of fact.

The fact was easily observable. Whereas certain aspects of human society were definitely mirrored in the animal world, *the major aspect was not.*

The clue had been provided long before by someone said simply: "Man is the religious animal". No one picked up this clue for a long time, and for obvious reasons. Religion was discredited by science, something agreed upon by liberals and the new biologists alike. Yet, in that simple statement was an immense biological truth, and a truth that might well have been unappreciated by whoever uttered it.

The fact of the matter was simply that animal behaviour, although it could *mirror* human and social behaviour, could not account for the complexity of human society and behaviour. Far from grasping at "special creation" straws to account for this, some of us worked to extend the work of the "new biologists" that Ardrey had popularized so well. We did not take the "liberal" stance of simply ignoring the facts, or of brusquely dismissing Ardrey as "unhumanitarian" or slandering Lorenz as a "Nazi". Some of us were not afraid of the Ardrey-Lorenz facts . . . what bothered us was that these facts did not explain the entire human situation.

The uniquely human complexity of behavior and society could be explained by proposing an extension of territorial behavior into another dimension never conceived by Ardrey or Lorenz . . . *time.*

Unlike any other human animal, human beings have conceived

of an existence for themselves which extends beyond the barriers of an individual's birth and death. Human beings, uniquely (so far as we know) among earth creatures, conceive of a human reality greater than any one lifetime. This greater existence, time itself extending into the past and future, was a new sort of territory ... an afterlife or a belief that some sort of human environment exists after an individual has passed out of the biological and material world. This belief is the simplest form of "religion". Religion is the recognition of a new type of territory, time, which human beings can inhabit after death from the material world.

Once we conceived of the new sort of human territory represented by time, we were forced to preserve those people who understood it, or claimed to understand it, to help the rest of us be a part of it. The first people preserved were shamans, priests who claimed to be able to communicate with the dead and who could describe "where" these dead had gone ... and where all of us would someday go. Shamans were valuable because they eased our own fear of death ... now that we understood it as no animal ever did before.

And the shaman was valuable for another reason, although we probably didn't appreciate it at the time many thousands of years ago. He/she was probably a bit more intelligent than the rest of us. A shaman may not have been a great warrior or hunter, and might have been a puny physical specimen, but the intelligence may have yielded a more acute perception of relationships. For instance, a shaman might have understood that if a hunter looked like a deer, the animal could be approached more closely and hunters would be successful more often. The first cave drawing of a shaman, at Les Trois Freres in France, does, in fact, show a man dressed in in a deer skin, wearing the antlers as a head-dress, and performing some sort of "magic", probably to ensure hunters' success.

And make no mistake about it, it *was* magic because such camouflage would miraculously increase the group's welfare by ensuring a greater probability of hunting success. The added "survival margin" gained by the shaman in this way allowed the group's security to be enhanced ... so that the group could preserve yet other people with exceptional intelligence. Once begun, this process became a geometric function of application of intelligence to human life. It was apparently primitive "priests" (but more probably "priestesses") who hit on the idea of agriculture, that food could be *planned* against future need, and their time-factored calendars were crucial to this planning. Labour could be divided for more efficiency, and *planning* could begin to be substituted for biological *reaction.*

The new territory of time could be asserted and defended only by the application of "extra" intelligence *that was of no great value in the purely biological world.* But this "extra" intelligence, accumulating geometrically through artificial preservation, began to account for human progress. Before the group preservation of exceptional intelligence, there was only one way of communicating with the future — through the biological creation of offspring. But once a sufficient surface-tension of excess intelligence had been accumulated, a purely intellectual way of storing information and communicating it to the future was devised: writing. In *The Cronos Complex* (1973), I defined writing as: *non-biological communication with the future.* It was a great step in human progress because the *results* of exeptional intelligence could be preserved, not just exceptionally intelligent people in their natural lifetimes.

There are plenty of ironies involved in the idea of a biological creature attempting to inhabit the non-biological environment of time. There are even more ironic repercussions when such a creature brings assertive and defensive territorial behaviour into the strange environment. It causes a great deal of confusion and psychological ambivalence in various areas of life. But one irony of humanity's territoriality in time is very relevant to this book: we have progressed as a race by the artificial preservation of individuals exhibiting exceptional intelligence, sensitivity, creativity.

The irony is that although humanity seems to be the most successful biological species, *its success has been due to the artificial preservation of biological failures.*

If we had evolved only according to the dictates of biological "survival of the fittest" we would still be in the cave ... we would just be stronger specimens of cave people.

These biological studies and conclusions led me to the

conclusion that no North American political party had an ideology that reflected the totality of human nature.

The "free-enterprisers" based their political and economic ideology only on the "survival of the fittest" imperative and ignored the co-operative and compassionate behaviour which had truly been responsible for our progress. The "socialists" were no better, since they based their ideal of co-operation and compassion on some rather inadequate theoretical construct while denying altogether the very real need for aggressive competition.

I looked in vain for a party which founded itself according to the totality of "human nature" (insofar as it is known) and was not afraid to structure political, economic and social programs appropriately . . . always leaving, if possible, margin for error and flexibility to accommodate future insights.

In theory, any party could decide to do this. But within the actual reality of contemporary Canada, only one political party might be able to change its ideology sufficiently to accommodate the facts of "human nature" as they are presently understood. This party is the NDP. It is the only party in Canada not irrevocably committed to the defence of an obsolescent and contracting economy and society. It could evolve into a true "people's party" in the sense that it reflects what the people really are, want and need.

But this evolution will require jettisoning some cherished ideological baggage . . . and it is anything but certain that the NDP can pass through the eye of the needle.

The baggage that must be abandoned is Marxism, not *only* because it has hopelessly tainted associations in North America, but, and more importantly, because it is an inadequate and inaccurate model of human behaviour.

I do not intend to digress into a detailed discussion of what Marx actually wrote, what has been correctly and incorrectly attributed to him, how all of that has been interpreted as society has changed since Marx died. I think that any such lengthy digression is unjustified simply because some inadequacies and inaccuracies of the Marxist model should be very apparent by now. These may be listed and briefly fleshed out:

1. Capitalism does not *cause* warfare ... although it fuels the fires since capitalism itself is a mechanism of aggressive expression and, of course, capitalism profits from the conflagration. The major cause of warfare is territorial assertion and defence. This behaviour is intimately associated with "identity".

2. Organized workers probably never did form a "class" in the sense that Marx apparently intended. Marx was greatly influenced by Darwin, and even wanted to dedicate *Capital* to him. Marx seems to use the term "class" in the same way that Darwin used the term "species" and Marx's idea of social evolution was something like a biotope in which these "classes" struggled for dominance and "evolved" human society in the process. European society was a highly stratified affair formed by age-old feudalism and 18th-19th Century industrialism was grafted onto that ... Marx can be forgiven for observing class distinctions that were so great that it was hard to imagine any way of bridging them. The fact remains that these classes were of the same *species* after all, and it did not take too long (only about 200 years) for "class'consciousness" to become well-blurred in modern Western Europe. It is doubtful if the workers of Western Europe are presently a "class" in the way that Marx meant.

   But workers in North America never formed a "class" in the partly-valid Marxist European perspective, and North American workers *never considered themselves such a class*. North American workers, as a group, have never shown any tendency to want to change the mainstream society in any fundamental way. Their goal has always been to gain greater economic franchise in the mainstream society.

3. Marxism exhibits little concern for the ground-up development of industry since it was assumed that the greed of the capitalists and their aggression-competition would take care of building industry. Socialists subsequently concerned themselves with the *distribution* processes of the economy, not the *productive* processes.

   Socialists are therefore in trouble if their capitalists have grown timid! The people, including workers, will be disadvantaged if the productive sector fails to provide adequate wealth to distribute. Marxist socialists have no ready-made ideology for *promoting* business competition...that was the capitalists' job in The Great Compromise.

4. Religion *has been used* as an "opiate of the masses", but it *is* not that *essentially,* as Marx said. Religion, in a biological sense, is a cultural adaptation responding to the conception of time as a territory, or environment, for human habitation. It is a perfectly valid recognition of Past-Present-Future human continuity and the understanding, compassion and co-operation that permits cultural sharing of this non-biological dimension. It was the way in which human beings first entered this dimension and provided biological havens for exceptional intelligence (priests, shamans, etc.). We have other ways of entering the territory of time now, but most of them grew out of "religion" not so long ago. It is no wonder that there is some confusion about what this non-biological dimension really is...is it a naive "heaven" which is eternal and non-aggressive where everyone plays harps and everyone is sweet? Or is it a *nirvana* where a soul can (and must) discard the patterns of assertion and defences of personality that were acquired during the time of biological and material competition?

"Religion", no matter how primitive or evolved, is an attempt to get a handle on this non-biological territory of time which is recognized to be "spiritual" in the sense that it is non-biological.

Religion has better biological credentials than Marxism.

If the New Democratic Party is to free itself of ideological fetters that compromise the validity of the policies it can develop, then the party must abandon Marxism as a guiding principle beneath "socialist" evolution. This will be a painful thing to do, too painful for some party members because Marxism has been like a favourite old shoe...it may be worn out and chafe the wearer on occasion, but it is comfortably familiar.

An integral part of abandoning Marxism must be the decision to cease official trade union affiliation...the very thing that David Lewis worked so hard to achieve. Yet it must be obvious that official trade union affiliation was a "Marxist automatic response" that had no validity at all within the North American social reality. Election after election has demonstrated that the majority of trade unionists do not vote for the NDP. The organized workers themselves, quite obviously, do not share the ideology, and are not about to assume the social role, that David Lewis's theoretical Marxism insisted they *must*. They don't. It is as simple as that.

This is not to say that the NDP should suddenly become "anti-union", though it may come to that as the defence of North American industry becomes more frantic. The NDP should regard trade unionists as individuals... people, not a "class" or "movement". Some trade unionists, perhaps the majority, are likely to vote the way their bread is buttered — for the Grits and Tories who are committed to the North American industrial status quo. But some trade union members, like members of any other sort of organization, will appreciate the fact that a stagnating industry and society must lower the quality of their lives even if they, personally, remain secure. Some of these people will vote NDP if the party can create policies that seem to offer an alternative to deepening industrial feudalism.

As mentioned previously in a Laxer quote, about 70% of the Canadian work force is employed in the "service sector", a very natural state of affairs for a branch-plant economy. These people are inclined to view the large and powerful unions associated with the basic smokestack industries with the gravest suspicions. These unions are not so much adversaries of the industrial system as they are partners in it. If North America slides into a sort of industrial feudalism on the obsolete smokestack industries, then the largest trade unions will be favoured vassals and supporters of the "capitalists". These trade unions can protect themselves against the worst effects of unemployment and inflation, while those in the service sector cannot.

The North American trade unions must be regarded as a conservative force, not a "radical" or progressive one, and the NDP's misapprehension that they could be anything else is the direct result of "automatic Marxist response" on the part of a few party intellectuals and organizers. Severing any official trade union ties, while welcoming individual union members who share the party's new ideology (along with everyone else who does so), will be regarded as a progressive development by the Canadian electorate.

Freed from Marxist doctrine, the party could begin to look at the Canadian predicament in a way that does not involve an automatic response that is dictated by an irrelevant ideology.

In 1983 Laxer suggested a "New Economic Strategy for Canada" in the final chapter of his *Rethinking the Economy*. His strategy was basically a defiance of the protection of obsolescent North American industry and refusal to accept Canada's vassal branch-plant status within a declining economic and social order. Laxer challenged the NDP to adopt a policy of rebuilding the Canadian industrial sector from the ground up. A mixture of public and private investment would be necessary. Strangely enough, according to Laxer, the funds are available. During this time of recession and inflation Canadians (always noted for being good savers) managed to *increase* their private savings to $68.03-*billion* in 1982. The problem has been to get Canadians to invest in their own country. Laxer proposes a "National Reguilding Fund", a special government bond issue, to mobilize this capital for building modern industries from the ground up. But this program cannot be a replay of earlier Canadian industrialization when the lion's share was conveniently located in Central Canada with very little for the West or the Maritimes.

> To make this a national effort, Canadians in the Atlantic provinces and the West must be fully involved. The rebuilding of the manufacturing sector will require such a major effort that it cannot succeed if it is seen as a replay of industrialization of the past — with manufacturing in Central Canada feeding off the rest of the country. . .
> . . . The money would be invested in productive sectors of the economy. It would be invested in publicly owned companies (new and existing), in joint ventures and in private companies. Some examples of where it could be invested would be: in high-technology manufacturing to promote and underwrite Canadian efforts in microelectronics and in communications equipment; in the establishment of a world scale mining machinery complex in Northern Ontario; in the building of a steel making and transportation equipment complex in the lower mainland of British Columbia; in the

development of petrochemical, petroleum machinery and agricultural equipment manufacturing in the Prairies; in the rebuilding of the aerospace industry in Quebec; and in the shipbuilding and fish-plant equipment industries in Atlantic Canada.[2]

In short, Laxer's national strategy involves the idea of making certain product categories in areas which have a natural domestic and local demand for a certain type of product. Laxer points out that although Canada is the third largest mining country in the world, we have a $1-billion trade deficit in mining equipment trade. We import mining equipment. We should be manufacturing it ourselves and even exporting it. This sort of story is the norm for all Canadian regions and industrial activity. We export the raw materials, but the extraction is accomplished with foreign-made equipment, the processing of the raw materials is done elsewhere.

Private corporations will be encouraged to invest by first raising the nominal corporate tax rate ... "and then lowering it to reward specific activities undertaken to upgrade the manufacturing sector." Laxer continues:

> ... If Canadian-owned (private) manufacturing companies were offered a choice, a high corporation tax if profits are not usefully reinvested, or a much lower one if useful investments are made, they will take the second choice. Companies should be given corporate tax points off if they purchase Canadian equipment, carry out research and development, deploy new and more productive techniques, train workers for skilled jobs, and encourage advancement for women.[3]

Laxer calls for stiff Canadian content requirements to be applied to branch-plants operating in Canada "based on the principle that if multinationals make a profit here, they must create jobs in Canada."

> ... The objective in key sectors should be: a dollar's worth of *production* (my italics) for every dollar spent by Canadians to purchase the products of the company.[4]

In short, Laxer advocates a frankly patriotic economic policy

which is unashamedly "Canada First"...just like Nixon's policies of August 15, 1971 were frankly protectionist, "patriotic"
and "America First". But Laxer's strategy incorporates an
important difference: it is a strategy for regaining the ability to
compete internationally, not to protect an obsolescent industrial
apparatus. Laxer would ask Canadians to commit to a determination to build a new industry, just like the post-war West
Europeans and Japanese managed to do, and to build a new type
of society at the same time.

Laxer's strategy is a radical departure from what might be
called "classical Marxist" socialism, and a radical departure from
the familiar NDP stance. His strategy is concerned with stimulating and rebuilding Canada's *productive* sector, not so much with
distributing the wealth from it. Laxer assumes, with good reason,
that such a strategy undertaken by *humanists* must build in
equitable distribution because that's the whole point of an
economy:

> The most basic choice of all concerns our view of human
> nature — of what motivates people and of what the pur-
> poses of social and economic organization should be.
>   In the final analysis, debates about economic strategy
> have always been debates about the kind of society we
> desire. In a conservative economic order, there is an ulti-
> mate distortion of means and ends. In it, the vast majority of
> people are means to the end of economic progress — with
> only a few titans being fully human actors. In a humanist
> economic order, the economy is a means, and nothing more
> than that, for the realization of human goals.[5]

Tommy Douglas might have written that, and Laxer's economic strategy resembles nothing so much as the Saskatchewan
CCF's industrial strategy between 1944 and 1961 except, of
course, that Laxer's emphasis is upon industry appropriate to the
end of the 20th Century rather than to the middle of it. It is also a
social and economic strategy which, *at last,* presupposes a generally co-operative and compassionate total structure, but one
incorporating a good deal of internal competition. It values
competition and individual contribution to the system, but does
not make aggession the basis of the construct.

In short, it is an outline for a social and economic structure which seems to approximate the "new biology's" data about human nature rather well . . . or, at least, much better than "survival of the fittest capitalism" defending an obsolete society and economy on one hand, and inadequate and inaccurate Marxist ideology on the other.

* * * * * *

The election of Brian Mulroney on September 4, 1984 confronts us all with a choice: are Canadians content to remain second-hand recipients of a declining economy and culture in North America, or are Canadians willing to stand up to create a new and more promising social and economic reality?

Is the sensible and responsible course of action acceptance of "successful surrender" (for some) to the Canadian predicaments, or a determination to challenge to inevitability of these predicaments?

In the past, Canadians have not shown much enthusiasm for their governments or for attempts to challenge the dictates of their predicaments.

Canadians have often had very little to be enthusiastic about. The country's basic predicaments seemed too large and insoluble, and the governments founded on the principle of appeasing and munipulating the regions have bred cynicism in Canadians even while wearily exchanging black cats for white ones. Canadians seem resigned to two facts: the country is too diverse to be pulled together for any great national purpose, and there is no political party they are about to trust out of long and bitter experience.

It is possible, however, that the world has been changing some of our predicaments for us by both good and bad developments happening around us. The regions are not so isolated as they once were. To some degree, modern communications technology has bridged the distances. The differing cultures and economic foundations of the regions remain . . . but these differences have been dwarfed by escalating dangers to us all. All Canadians have a direct stake in world peace, and a direct stake in a clean environment. Nuclear escalation and environmental pollution render some of our most cherished, and divisive, regional differences very petty indeed.

If we are to succumb to the temptations of "successful surrender" and cheerfully become a small part of a contracting North American society and economy, then we may be surrendering more than we thought. On May 14, 1985 the Tories released their Green Paper called *Directions for Canada's International Relations* which gently introduced the changes anticipated by Laxer. The 43-page document prepared by the Mulroney government was "the Tories' first formal effort to reshape Canada's foreign policy since taking power in September. It is also the first full scale public review of foreign policy since 1970." In brief, the Tories' Green Paper suggested strengthened ties with the United States and possibly a special free-trade pact. An increase in the defence budget was also suggested, although massive investment in America's "Star Wars" (Strategic Defence Initiative) program was left for future consideration. The economic policy of "free-trade", which can only be one way in a branch-plant economy, came as no special surprise and had been predicted by everyone and hinted by Mulroney two months earlier. But the increased defence budget and hedging about Star Wars can only be an ominous portent for the future. Is the price of American "trade" a demand that Canada should become a more significant purchaser of U.S. weapons? That seems to be the way the wind is blowing. Canada will nudge into the U.S. military orbit even more. The Green Paper also suggested a slashed foreign aid program and reduced contact with the Third World.

Canada has begun the process of alignment with the United States in a pact of North American neo-isolationism protected by defence increases and continental trade agreements. But the apparent pressure on Canada to increase defence spending means not only that Canada's trade with the U.S. will increase even more (it is presently almost 75% of Canada's total trade), but that we will be contributing to the destabilization of world peace by supporting the U.S. arms industry. As Val Sears wrote in the *Toronto Star* in May 1985:

Gone are the days when Canada was a "helpful fixer" on the international scene under Pearson, a Nobel Peace Prize winner; gone as well are Trudeau's North-South and peace initiatives.

The Mulroney Doctrine now requires Canada to make the best deals possible in a world we cannot influence.

"Successful surrender" may not prove to be security at all, even in short-sighted terms and much less in the longer term. In addition to draining the economy through "free-trade", increasing our participation in making the world less secure, The Mulroney Doctrine may be the death-knell of Canada's independent identity. The loss of Canadian identity may seem unimportant to some of us who have grown cynical about the quality of our governments and the quality of our culture, and this sort of identity has, in any case, too often been associated with a narrow "nationalism" that has caused much harm in the world. But, nonetheless, this intangible, "identity", seems very important to Canadians. Against great odds of geographic, cultural and political predicaments, Canadians have held their country together somehow, although at great cost in cultural and economic "compromises" that have impoverished the quality of their lives.

The fact that this intangible, "identity", has proved to be important to Canadians would not come as a surprise to a "new biologist". Organisms strive for "identity", because identity is *relevance*. In biological terms, this relevance is demonstrated by reproduction and the ability of an organism to influence the future in the only way available in the purely biological world. But even though this "striving for relevance" is *demonstrated* by reproductive success and is *expressed* through various mechanisms of territorial behaviour, it seems to *be* something else. Even animals do not appear to be simple mechanisms operating wholly by biological response. There is something else at work, but no one has been able to isolate it and describe it from laboratory experiments. Scientists have had glimpses.

Very interesting experiments have shown that animals will persist in territorial behaviour to the last extremity, long after any possibility of biological reproduction has been removed and up to the threshold of death itself. In 1949 a behavioural researcher named J.C. Braddock, working with platys, a common aquarium fish, showed that they would continue to assert and defend their territories, their means of expressing relevance, as the temperature of the water was lowered. The water would become too cold for them to breed, too cold for them to eat, too cold for them to live... and they died asserting and defending their territories. Similar experiments, many thousands of them, have revealed the same tendency in most species of animals. The territorial imperative has reproductive relevance, but it is not simply a biological-reproductive mechanism. For individuals, the need to be "relevant", to have an identity, is the most important thing in life. This "intangible" persists to motivate when there is no biological-reproductive way of influencing the future.

For Braddock's platys, their prediaments imposed successive limitations leading to death itself, but their final expression was the assertion of "identity"... which seems to be a drive to be relevant to the future, even if that drive cannot find actual expression. Perhaps this curious drive is what pushes life to evolve, what created life in the first place.

So it is not surprising that Canadians should have retained a determination to preserve their identity as a nation, in spite of their colonial history and their predicaments. This intangible identity-drive is likely to be the last, and most powerful, motivator of Canadians as a social unit... long after they have given in to temptations of short-sighted economic "security" represented by The Mulroney Doctrine. In the end, they will want to be "relevant to the future", just like platys in chilling water. After four years of Tory "successful surrender", Canadians as a social unit may have realized that what is being surrendered is any possibility that they can be "relevant to the future", and they will fight for *that*... like platys in a cold aquarium.

The next four years, from now until the election of 1988, provides the NDP with an unparalleled opportunity for achieving political relevance itself. The Mulroney Doctrine demonstrates clearly that there is now no real difference between the Liberal and the Conservative parties... they both represent a fear of the future and a cynicism which has compromised Canadian potential for being relevant to the future. And they always have. In following the path of least resistance in 1985, Mulroney's Tories are merely re-asserting the Liberal's policy of 1945 when Canada's branch-plant economy was created. This cannot escape the notice of voters.

If Canadians can see a real alternative to their loss of identity, they will take it. If they can trust a political party, they will follow its policy for assuring relevance to the future. At least, a significant minority will follow such a party and policy in 1988. Perhaps even a majority.

But presently there is no such alternative, and no such party to follow. The NDP's internal inconsistencies have made it untrustworthy.

Earlier in this book I related the historical development of organizations such as the Templars, Masons, and De Molay society, and their influence on the "humanist" thought in the new world, and how persons, such as the young Tommy Douglas, were drawn to their teachings. There is no doubt that Tommy Douglas was influenced a great deal in his youth by the precepts of the De Molay society — public service and human commitment. These were ideals which he carried with him into political life — ideals which greatly molded the original precepts of the CCF. This "humanist" platform is what made believers of ordinary Canadian voters...voters who in turn gave the CCF its clearest mandate, and its greatest political successes. Unfortunately, this political commitment has been lost with the passing of Douglas, and other CCF founders, from the political scene. In its place came the "British Labour-style" socialist platform of David Lewis and other eastern socialists...and consequently the continued erosion of grass roots popularity of the NDP.

It is obvious that the founding ideals of the NDP have become dulled and need to be revitalized. The ideals of humanism and political compassion, originally such a radical advance over the European socialist stasis, have evolved into structures betraying their founding spirit. The ideal of "equal opportunity" in Canada has evolved through free-enterprise competition into a situation in which a few huge multinational corporations have emerged as victors in the economic jungle. Merger mania has consolidated this system even more in recent years. What is emerging is an economic feudalism that is anything but free and offers anything but opportunities for individual competition. It is becoming a system dominated by a few corporate giants in which ordinary people have decreasing input and in which new business has scant chance of survival. In short, the original potential of the North American social experiment is becoming compromised.

Perhaps it is time for the NDP to re-evaluate its continued

adherence to the platform which has led to its decline over the past 40 years. What was in there in the original beliefs of the CCF which brought it to the brink of majority in Canada? Beliefs which people responded to — a goal seeking an essentially compassionate and humane society.

Bibliography

Chapter Two

1. McCall Newman, Christina, *Grits*, Macmillan of Canada, Toronto, 1982, page 387.
2. *Grits*, page 388.
3. *Grits*, page 256.
4. MacDonald, Ian L., *Mulroney The Making of the Prime Minister*, McClelland and Stewart, Toronto, 1984, page 298.
5. *Mulroney The Making of the Prime Minister*, page 12.
6. *Mulroney The Making of the Prime Minister*, page 194.
7. *Mulroney The Making of the Prime Minister*, page 30.
8. *Mulroney The Making of the Prime Minister*, page 31.
9. *Mulroney The Making of the Prime Minister*, page 116.

Chapter Three

1. Shackleton, Doris French, *Tommy Douglas*, McClelland and Stewart, Toronto, 1975, page 17.
2. *Tommy Douglas*, page 17.
3. *Tommy Douglas*, page 26.
4. McNaught, K., "J.S. Woodsworth and a Political Party for Labour, 1896-1921", *Canadian Historical Review*, 1949, (mss 61).
5. *Tommy Douglas*, page 298.
6. *Tommy Douglas*, page 28.
7. *Tommy Douglas*, page 30.
8. *Tommy Douglas*, page 32.
9. *Tommy Douglas*, page 32.
10. *Tommy Douglas*, page 31.
11. *Tommy Douglas*, page 32.
12. *Tommy Douglas*, page 52.
13. *Tommy Douglas*, page 53.
14. *Tommy Douglas*, page 54.
15. *Tommy Douglas*, page 64-65.
16. *Tommy Douglas*, page 125.
17. *Tommy Douglas*, page 123.
18. *Tommy Douglas*, page 110.
19. *Tommy Douglas*, page 111.
20. *Tommy Douglas*, page 113-114.

21. *Tommy Douglas*, page 116-117.
22. *Tommy Douglas*, page 121.
23. *Tommy Douglas*, page 121.
24. *Tommy Douglas*, page 128.
25. *Tommy Douglas*, page 123.
26. *Tommy Douglas*, page 123.
27. *Tommy Douglas*, page 124.
28. *Tommy Douglas*, page 127.
29. *Tommy Douglas*, page 127.
30. *Tommy Douglas*, page 160.
31. *Tommy Douglas*, page 160.
32. *Tommy Douglas*, page 161.
33. *Tommy Douglas*, page 182.
34. *Tommy Douglas*, page 181.
35. *Tommy Douglas*, page 181.
36. *Tommy Douglas*, page 233.
37. *Tommy Douglas*, page 233.
38. *Tommy Douglas*, page 235.
39. *Tommy Douglas*, page 237.
40. *Tommy Douglas*, page 240.
41. Baigent, Michael, et al., *The Holy Blood and the Holy Grail*, Jonathon Cape, London, 1982, page 85.
42. *The Holy Blood and the Holy Grail*, page 36-65.
43. *The Holy Blood and the Holy Grail*, page 49.

Chapter Four

1. *Tommy Douglas*, page 287.
2. *Tommy Douglas*, page 27.
3. Koestler, Arthur, *The Thirteenth Tribe*, Hutchinson & Co. (Publishers) Ltd., London, 1976, all information about Shtetls and Khazaria from Koestler's book.
4. Lewis, David. *The Good Fight*, Macmillan of Canada, Toronto, 1981, page 14.
5. *The Good Fight*, page 14.
6. *The Good Fight*, page 32.
7. *The Good Fight*, page 35-36.
8. *The Good Fight*, page 1.
9. *The Good Fight*, page 37.
10. *The Good Fight*, page 44.
11. *The Good Fight*, page 65.
12. *The Good Fight*, page 71.
13. *The Good Fight*, page 74.
14. *The Good Fight*, page 56-57.
15. *The Good Fight*, page 75.
16. *The Good Fight*, page 75.
17. *The Good Fight*, page 75-76.
18. *The Good Fight*, page 80.
19. *The Good Fight*, page 85.
20. *The Good Fight*, page 85.
21. *The Good Fight*, page 81.

22. *The Good Fight*, page 110.
23. *The Good Fight*, page 111.
24. *The Good Fight*, page 111.
25. *The Good Fight*, page 111.
26. *The Good Fight*, page 110.
27. *The Good Fight*, "The Gestapo Affair", page 270 to 287.
28. *The Good Fight*, page 266.
29. *The Good Fight*, page 302.
30. *The Good Fight*, page 495.
31. *The Good Fight*, page 495.
32. *The Good Fight*, page 249.
33. *The Good Fight*, page 496.
34. *Tommy Douglas*, page 249.
35. *Tommy Douglas*, page 247-248.
36. *Tommy Douglas*, page 250.
37. *Tommy Douglas*, page 174-175.
38. *Tommy Douglas*, page 315.
39. *Tommy Douglas*, page 270.
40. *Tommy Douglas*, page 290-291.
41. *Tommy Douglas*, page 291.
42. *Tommy Douglas*, page 308.
43. *Tommy Douglas*, page 308-309.
44. *Tommy Douglas*, page 293.
45. *Tommy Douglas*, page 293.
46. Stewart, Walter, "The Touch, Lonely Man in the Middle", *Star Weekly*, January 8, 1966.
47. *The Good Fight*, page 506-507.

Chapter Five

1. Laxer, James, *Rethinking the Economy*, N. C. Press Limited, Toronto, 1983, page 31.
2. *Rethinking the Economy*, page 31.
3. *Rethinking the Economy*, page 60.
4. *Rethinking the Economy*, page 102-103, 106.
5. *Rethinking the Economy*, page 103-106.

Chapter Six

1. *Rethinking the Economy*, page 135.
2. *Rethinking the Economy*, page 124, 126, (... Atlantic Canada., mss 377).
3. *Rethinking the Economy*, page 128, (... for women., mss 378).
4. *Rethinking the Economy*, page 129, (... of the company., mss 378).
5. *Rethinking the Economy*, page 138, (... of human goals., mss 379).